HOW CULTURAL DIFFERENCES SHAPE THE RECEPTION OF KNOWLEDGE

HOW CULTURAL DIFFERENCES
SHAPE THE RECEPTION OF KNOWLEDGE
A Psychology of Learning and Teaching
for Democratic Societies

A.P. Craig

The Edwin Mellen Press
Lewiston•Queenston•Lampeter

Library of Congress Cataloging-in-Publication Data

Craig, A. P. (Anita P.)
  How cultural differences shape the reception of knowledge : a psychology of
learning and teaching for democratic societies / A.P. Craig.
    p. cm.
  Includes bibliographical references and index.
  ISBN-13: 978-0-7734-5714-0
  ISBN-10: 0-7734-5714-3
  1. Learning, Psychology of. 2. Cognitive learning. I. Title.
  LB1060.C725 2007
  370.15'23--dc22

                                                         2007002750

hors serie

A CIP catalog record for this book is available from the British Library.

Front Cover: Joh's final year at school (1931). Author's mother (front row, centre). Family photo.

All rights reserved. For information contact
          The Edwin Mellen Press   The Edwin Mellen Press
                Box 450   Box 67
          Lewiston, New York   Queenston, Ontario
          USA 14092-0450   CANADA L0S 1L0

                    The Edwin Mellen Press, Ltd.
                    Lampeter, Ceredigion, Wales
                    UNITED KINGDOM SA48 8LT

            Printed in the United States of America

For Koto-Maxx and the rest of Piet and Joh's great-grand line

TABLE OF CONTENTS

LIST OF ILLUSTRATIONS

PREFACE

The sciences of mind and brain have enjoyed a sustained and accelerating period of growth and excitement for most of the past 50 years. Most of what has been discovered is directly relevant to what happens in the classroom. Nonetheless it has had very little impact on the ways in which teachers are trained, including in South Africa. This should stop: teachers should be seen as applied cognitive scientists, and trained accordingly. That, in a nutshell, is what seems to me to be Anita Craig's most general argument in this work. I agree with that general argument, although differing with Craig on some other levels.

The pace of discovery in cognitive science for the past 20 or so of those years has been especially astonishing as a wide range of very powerful and unprecedented technologies have arisen, matured and helped set the agenda. Among these technologies are artificial neural networks, allowing the construction and manipulation of computing systems more clearly inspired by actual brain microanatomy than any previous human invention, and functional magnetic resonance imaging, allowing the changing distribution of brain activity during the performance of a task to be measured. But there is much, much more. Comparative studies of the cognitive properties of different species have multiplied, illuminating our understanding of ourselves considerably. The long tradition of experimentation in cognitive psychology has differentiated and matured in a variety of ways, and formed striking coalitions with new players like brain scanning, or older ones like behavioural ecology. Despite the lousy and unfair press they regularly receive (including the extraordinary myth that an entire research programme was vanquished by a single very sarcastic book review) behaviourists have continued to amass a wealth of data of unrivalled precision, organised by increasingly subtle and sophisticated theories,[1] about the influence of economic factors on the allocation of resources by living systems. Behaviourists too have found more recent playmates, in such hybrid fields as behavioural economics and neuroeconomics.

Almost all of this has at least some relevance to, and is often directly about, what happens (or is supposed to happen) in the classroom. That is, the cognitive sciences have studied and continue to study, among other things, the acquisition of knowledge and skills, the processes that can accelerate and impede that acquisition, the prerequisites for it, and related processes of retrieval, maintenance, loss of skill and knowledge. Only a small fraction of what has been discovered is unsurprising. Here are a very few randomly chosen examples. A significant fraction of attentive subjects counting the passes of a ball between a group of people on a video screen will fail to notice a person in a gorilla suit who walks to the middle of the group, stares at the camera for a few seconds, and then walks away.[2] Talking to yourself, rather than being a 'sign of insanity', is a feature of the learning of those who learn most quickly and well.[3] The brain regions subserving the maintenance of semantic and lexical information about tools are not the same as those for information about animals.[4] Similarly, there are

---

[1] See, for example, Rachlin, H., *The Science of Self-control* (Cambridge, MA: Harvard University Press, 2000); also, Ainslie, G., *Breakdown of Will* (Cambridge: CUP, 2001).
[2] Simons, D.J. and Chabris, C.F., 'Gorillas in our midst: Sustained inattentional blindness for dynamic events', *Perception*, 28 (1999), 1059–74.
[3] See, for example, Berk, L. and Garvin, R., 'Development of private speech among low-income Appalachian children', *Developmental Psychology*, 20/2 (1984), 271–86; Bivens, J. and Berk, L.A., 'A longitudinal study of the development of elementary school children's private speech', *Merrill-Palmer Quarterly*, 36/4 (1990), 443–63. Even now, in 2006, I find that a significant proportion of the year's first-year students have been told that any self-directed speech is a psychological symptom.
[4] See, for example, Damasio, H., Grabowski, T.J., Tranel, D., Hichwa, R.D. and Damasio, A.R., 'A neural basis for lexical retrieval', *Nature*, 380 (1996), 449–505.

cases in which everyday objects cannot be recognised by sight, but can when touched.[5] When an animal, including a human one, learns to use a tool for reaching, part of the neural representation, in its brain, of its own hand is 'mapped' onto the representation of the part of space at the end of the tool.[6] Males who have looked at pictures of attractive females are temporarily more sensitive to delay than otherwise.[7]

This wealth of discovery and accompanying theory has, as far as I can tell, little impact on how teachers are trained, or educational policy formed. I make this claim not, I note, as one in the business of frequent and careful study of the curricula of the institutions that train teachers. It is a good ten years since I last enquired into what one learned in order to be allowed to teach. Then, though, it *certainly* wasn't cognitive science or indeed, as far as I could tell, any science relevant to learning or teaching at all. In my occasional encounters with what are supposed to be experts on education I all too often (although not always) find that they announce allegiance to this or that 'theory' much as some assert allegiance to a sports team. That is, they express loyalty rather than the conclusion of a process of considered judgement.[8] At least some avowed 'constructivists', for example, seem unwilling or even unable to get into a discussion of whether the phenomenon of path dependence in some kinds of learning is a serious problem for their orientation, if they've heard of path dependence in learning at all. Depressingly few of the experts or teachers seem even to have heard of cognitive science.[9]

---

[5] There are more bizarre and instructive types of agnosia than you can shake a stick at. Any good cognitive neuroscience textbook will survey some of them. For example, Gazzaniga, M.S., Ivry, R.B. and Mangun, G.R., *Cognitive Neuroscience* (New York: Norton, 2002).
[6] Maravita, A. and Iriki, A., 'Tools for the body (schema)', *Trends in Cognitive Science*, 8/2 (2004), 79–86.
[7] Wilson, M. and Daly, M., 'Do pretty women inspire men to discount the future?', *Proceedings of the Royal Society of London, Supplementary – Biology Letters* (2003), 271, S177–9.
[8] For a fine account of the poverty of reasoning skills, including among many of the supposedly educated, see Kuhn, D., *The Skills of Argument* (Cambridge: CUP, 1991).
[9] This is not a failing peculiar to the field of education in South Africa. I recently attended an economics conference, and saw a presentation in which those present were exhorted to 'go cognitive', which for the speaker apparently amounted to 'abandoning rationality'! Anyone

Notice how in some other fields a comparable innocence of moderately recent discovery would be regarded as no less than scandalous. A doctor who persisted in attributing stomach ulcers to 'stress' and prescribed accordingly, given the demonstration some years ago now that they are caused by infections, would be guilty of malpractice. That is, we *expect* our doctors, and others, to pay attention to what is discovered in their field by medical science after they qualify. For those who teach, the sciences of learning are (whether they or policy makers realise this) their field, and to the extent that Craig is calling on us to let this inform how teachers are trained and expected to behave in their ongoing work, I'm all for it.

On some more specific questions, I'm less clearly aligned with Craig's proposal. Before saying something about this, I note that I'm a philosopher by training, and although the greater part of my teaching and research is in cognitive science, I'm not an enemy of philosophy. I mention this because I don't want to give the wrong impression when I say that it seems to me as though the medicine Craig prescribes in the third chapter of her book contains too much philosophy.

Cognitive science is a fast moving, and in many ways new, field. Although some empirical results are very well established, our understanding of the mechanisms underlying much cognitive processing is in a state of flux, and there are serious theoretical disputes over what sorts of mechanisms the current data and state of theory suggest in many areas.[10] Anyone who wants to know the state of our scientific knowledge about learning and knowing, must be alert to this ongoing and active debate. So when Craig urges that it would be irresponsible to pick some theory off the shelf (whether Piaget, or Vygotsky, or whatever) and 'apply it in the classroom', I have to agree again.

In fact, while I'm being so agreeable, let me also say that I think the broad set of issues about situated cognition and the like that Craig lays out are among the

---

convinced by Craig's overall argument has some tough questions about implementation and the steepness of the hill that needs to be climbed to ask both her and themselves.

[10] Look at the articles in current issues of *Trends in Cognitive Science*, or read the spirited debate in the peer commentaries on a recent target article in *Behavioral and Brain Sciences* to get a sense of what I'm referring to.

ones that should inform any attempt to work out where the teaching professions might be advised to drop lines into the ocean of cognitive science. Where I *disagree* is over how important the questions that Jerry Fodor (a philosopher) cares about so much really are to cognitive science or teaching. Indeed it is not my impression that any useful partitioning of the practitioners of cognitive science is achieved by the four questions (about propositional attitudes, functionalism and truth-conditions) that Fodor proposes.[11] And while I (sort of) agree with Fodor's reasons for thinking that psychology does not reduce to neuropsychology, I think that the majority of the really interesting and important recent work in cognitive science actually *is* the brain science – especially cognitive neuroscience.[12]

This isn't the right place, though, to develop a competing version of the priorities. The fact that I'd urge more behaviourism and more neuroscience in the mix than Craig seems to suggest (certainly more than Fodor thinks important) is, perhaps, a symptom of some of the tensions and disputes that Craig is urging that you need to be aware of to get something useful out of cognitive science. And the really important point here, from which we shouldn't get distracted, is that there is plenty to be gained from cognitive science by the field of education.

Professor David Spurrett

School of Philosophy and Ethics
University of KwaZulu-Natal
Durban, South Africa

---

[11] While you're looking at the articles in current issues of *Trends in Cognitive Science*, as I suggested you do in the previous note, you can try (although I really don't suggest this) to use Fodor's questions to organise what you find. Answers on a postcard.

[12] Gazzaniga, Ivry, and Mangun, *Cognitive Neuroscience*.

FOREWORD

I want this book to serve as a *resource* for teachers in training, for Faculties and for Schools of Education. As such, I hope it will be used to open questions and issues about education, and to point discussions about how to improve on schooling, in general, and mass education, in particular. I do not think of this input as presenting teachers with a clear set of theories, principles and facts to apply without further ado to classroom problems. Rather, I hope that in working through my criticisms of what typically goes for 'education', and in reaching into the supply of answers I offer to some of the pressing problems that beset education, teachers and teachers of teachers will reorientate themselves as far as their central task goes.

I believe that it is time to save education, in general, from the sea of relativism into which too much of the thinking and doing crucial to our lives and regulative ideals has plunged. In particular, I am of the opinion that in deciding what to believe and how to live, a surer grasp of knowledge and applied knowledge will serve our projects well. Furthermore, I believe that the obvious knowledge base for learning (and teaching) is the study of cognition. These shifts, I think, will go some way towards redirecting education, as a discipline, so that schooling will deliver globally competitive products.

The particular questions I think worth considering are, briefly, about: (a) what the world offers and demands from participants, (b) education's central task, and (c) the demands of mass education. Important issues to consider involve: (d) the nature of learning, and (e) the differences between us. It is towards addressing these questions and issues that I present *the study of cognition* as central to teacher training.

These themes – thinking and acting in the world nowadays; education, in general, and mass education's central task; and learning and the differences between us – are tabled *again and again* throughout the book, each time from a different theoretical or practical angle. I do this both to avoid offering simple solutions to a very complex, and interrelated, set of problems, and to illustrate what I mean by applied cognition.

The book is made up of two parts: the first consists of an examination of education and, in particular, the thesis that the proper focus of mass schooling is on universally standardised skills, technology and knowledge; the second consists of an outline of the possibilities for the application of cognitive science to education. Both education and cognitive science are, however, highly contested fields, which mean that some of this has to show itself in what follows.

ACKNOWLEDGEMENTS

The first and most important tribute goes to colleagues and students involved in TTT (Durban), POLP (Cape Town), and the NDT project (Amsterdam); then to Carol MacDonald and Jos Beishuizen for acting as referees, to David Spurrett for writing the Preface and, as always, to Dylan Craig for lending me his native-speaker's eye and ear before final editing.

CHAPTER 1

Introduction

In this chapter I consider whether mass education can be excellent and, a related question, how this excellence can be found and maintained. In addition, I trace the thinking that led to all the relativism[1] around, and consider three specific views on education by way of framing the book as a whole.

Mass education, i.e. free or state-subsidised, compulsory education provided in state-run schools[2] for everybody over a certain age, constitutes a distinct break from the older, often religious, model favouring particular, selected groups or elites, in typically structured or hierarchical societies. Mass or universal education is also not all that old: it is a decade or so less than 300 years since the start of this programme in Germany under Friedrich Wilhelm,[3] and it is much younger still in, for example, some African democracies. The move to mass education is mostly thought of as a certain sacrifice in the name of a greater good. The sacrifice seemingly involves having to give up on superior aims and clear goals (e.g. excellence) and appropriate standards for measuring and attaining these (i.e. success through merit alone) in order to fulfil, in practice, greater goods such

---

[1] 'Relativism' indicates an explicit defence of the importance of considering the *context* of claims in their assessment; more about this in the rest of the chapter and Chapter 2.

[2] Generally I mean by 'schools' and related words the public places where children (roughly between four/five and 18 years of age, or from their first entry into state-controlled education to the end of their formal schooling) receive their education.

[3] Cf. http://www.findarticles.com/p/articles/mi_m2185/is_3_14/ai_99430630/print .

as democratic ideals. The latter, typically, is thought to involve equal treatment for all citizens, and their free and open access to basic rights such as education. Pitting these educational aims and goals *against* socio-political ideals is, however, not a productive way of thinking about education. And from another (Marxian) angle, I also do not think it useful to think of mass education as nothing more than a skill-supply factory for maintaining economic or class divisions in society.

I am of the opinion that mass education makes its own demands on teacher training and the skills, technology and knowledge focused on within the classroom, and that it has its own form of excellence.

Defining 'excellence' is not easy though. Where the standards by which something is to be evaluated, judged, or measured are certain or even absolute the highest achievement measured against these could be called excellent, but in cases where the standards are debatable or unclear, such praise is often debatable too. Moreover, since *excellence* has been pitted against *relevance* from about the 1960s onwards, specifically regarding education, excellence has become, for some, the suspect aim of exclusive institutions bent on remaining closed to change – such as the entry of 'others' (e.g. women, people of colour), or the intrusion of alien values, aims, and so forth.[4]

I will argue that excellence is to be understood in terms of the success with which schooling equips learners with *control over the code*. This is obviously a slightly defiant way of capturing the heart of the matter, and before clarifying and defending this, suffice it to say that by 'the code' I mean universally standardised

---

[4] Toulmin, S., *Cosmopolis. The Hidden Agenda of Modernity* (New York: The Free Press, 1990), 184–5, writes about the terms of this debate as follows: 'Pitting relevance against excellence redirected attention to the practical, local, transitory, and context bound issues that were close to the heart of the 16th-century humanists, but were set aside by 17th-century rationalists for abstract, timeless, universal and context free issues'. I have commented before on Toulmin's sentiments specifically regarding the developing world and do not wish to repeat this here. See Craig, A.P., 'Knowledge and democracy', *South African Journal of Higher Education*, 13/1 (1999), 18–30; and Craig, A.P., 'Really virtual/Virtually real', in Bensusan, D. (ed.), *W(h)ither the University* (Kenwyn: Juta and Co. Ltd, 1996), 62–73.

skills, technology, and knowledge, and by 'control over' I mean the cognitive wherewithal to know, use, and change these as each wills and is able.

In the rest of the chapter I describe some of the influences that got us into all the relativist, multiculturalist, postmodern, and other fashionable talk, and consider what is worth saving from all of this. I conclude the chapter with three stories about education by way of framing the analyses in the rest of the book.

1.1 Some of the water in the sea

The '60s were alive with the Hippies, communism in Europe, and liberations of different kinds (claimed by women, through student revolts, and from colonial powers); also with the voices of spokespeople for reclaimed identities and education for liberation, such as Franz Fanon[5] and Paulo Freire,[6] who inspired a generation of educators often far away from their own locales. The politics of recognition,[7] which in its turn depends on, and gives further impetus to, a resistance to universalising discourses such as western hegemony and male power, placed a number of issues on the agenda of public talk and political action. Examples include calls for equality between people – regardless of differences, or while specifically underlining such differences – and the accompanying demand for recognition of states of being 'other' than white, European, and male. Since the '60s, too, we have noted the increasing participation in the talk of the times by the previously excluded (the latter often related to the actual liberation of specific groups from the conditions of their oppression). All of these seem to be obvious

---

[5] Cf. http://www.epistemelinks.com/Main/Philosophers.aspx?PhilCode=Fano ;
http://www.marxists.org/reference/subject/philosophy/works/ot/fanon.htm ;
http://www.pipeline.com/~rgibson/FANON.htm .
[6] Cf. http://www.zonalatina.com/Zldata288.htm ;
http://www.findarticles.com/p/articles/mi_qa3935/is_200304/ai_n9181266#continue ;
http://www.findarticles.com/p/search?qt=paulo+freire&qf=free&tb=art .
[7] Cf. Appiah, K.A. and Gutmann, A., *Color Conscious. The Political Morality of Race* (Princeton, NJ: Princeton University Press, 1996); Goodhart, D., 'Too diverse?', *Prospect* (February 2004), 30–37; and Guttman, A. (ed.), *Multiculturalism* (Princeton, NJ: Princeton University Press, 1994).

4

gains and clear *social* goods, were it not also for the problems occasioned by differences in shared sites of exchange; more about this shortly.

Global mobility (for better or worse, depending on whether the émigrés have something to exchange or something to flee from) across national borders ensures that we often live nowadays in societies of strangers.[8] This part of globalisation[9] does seem to bring particular psychological pressures to bear on people living in such societies (the prominence of identity politics might be one symptom of this). Living with strangers or among different others further shows itself in tensions between conflicting commitments and identifications, beliefs, values, and strong evaluations (i.e. those evaluations people live for, and are also willing to die and kill for).

The politics of recognition, global mobility, and multicultural societies made up of a plurality of often conflicting orientations, values, and so forth, are accompanied by an almost world-wide resistance to single universal authorities, of whatever kind, and a certain resistance to the older 'melting pot'[10] vision regarding integration as a solution to differences in conflict. This means that it is not clear how to focus and direct the business of those sites deliberately left or

---

[8] 'The diversity, individualism and mobility that characterise developed economies – especially in the era of globalisation – mean that more of our lives is spent among strangers. Ever since the invention of agriculture 10,000 years ago, humans have been used to dealing with people from beyond their own extended kin groups. The difference now in a developed country like Britain is that we not only live among strangers but must share with them.' Goodhart, 'Too diverse?', 30–37.
[9] Giddens, A., *The Consequences of Modernity* (Cambridge: Polity Press, 1992).
[10] Booth, W., 'One nation, indivisible: Is it history?', *Washington Post* (22 February 1998); note the following from this: 'At the beginning of this century, as steamers poured into American ports, their steerages filled with European immigrants, a Jew from England named Israel Zangwill penned a play whose story line has long been forgotten, but whose central theme has not. His production was entitled "The Melting Pot" and its message still holds a tremendous power on the national imagination – the promise that all immigrants can be transformed into Americans, a new alloy forged in a crucible of democracy, freedom and civic responsibility.' http://www.washingtonpost.com/wp-srv/national/longterm/meltingpot/melt0222.htm .

made open and accessible to all or, in fact, made compulsory (as in the case of schooling[11]).

One part of the difficulty with differences is notable in the case of the banning of 'conspicuous religious symbols' in public schools,[12] another in arguments about the place of evolution in the school curriculum,[13] and yet another in discussions of the rights of gay teachers and whether gay people should even be allowed to be teachers.[14] That is to say, living with differences shows itself in conflicts between different commitments and identifications, beliefs, values and strong evaluations. An understandable response to these has been a series of attempts to waylay or cope with conflict, when this emerges, by preaching and promoting tolerance and some form of (cultural) relativism or multiculturalism. I think that these are laudable political, social and civic projects, but hopeless as a framing ideology for formal, mass schooling.

All the talk of, and even the lauding of, differences, as well as the various resistances briefly outlined, have been given a specific configuration in postmodern talk and its evaluation of pre-modern and different ways of knowing,

---

[11] I will not repeat some of the ludicrous attempts to make various subjects multicultural or responsive to differences. See Gardner, H., 'The New New Math', *New York Review of Books*, 45/14 (24 September 1998) and especially note the following: '"Ethnomathematics" is another popular word. It refers to math as practised by cultures other than Western, especially among primitive African tribes. A book much admired by fuzzy-math teachers is Marcia Ascher's *Ethnomathematics: A Multicultural View of Mathematical Ideas* (1991) ... "Critical-mathematical literacy" is an even longer jawbreaker. It appears in the NCTM [National Council of Teachers of Mathematics] yearbook as a term for the ability to interpret statistics correctly ... Knowing how pre-industrial cultures, both ancient and modern, handled mathematical concepts may be of historical interest, but one must keep in mind that mathematics, like science, is a cumulative process that advances steadily by uncovering truths that are everywhere the same. Native tribes may symbolize numbers by using different base systems, but the numbers behind the symbols are identical. Two elephants plus two elephants makes four elephants in every African tribe, and the arithmetic of these cultures is a miniscule portion of the vast jungle of modern mathematics.'
[12] The BBC reported on 2 September 2004 that 'A law banning Islamic headscarves and other religious symbols from French state schools came into effect on Thursday, the first day of term'. http://news.bbc.co.uk/1/hi/world/europe/3619988.stm . Cf. http://islam.about.com/cs/currentevents/i/france_hijab.htm .
[13] Cf. http://www.cnn.com/US/9908/12/kansas.evolution.flap/ .
[14] Cf. http://www.abanet.org/irr/hr/yared.html ; http://www.tes.co.uk/section/staffroom/thread.aspx?story_id=2068824&path=/scotland/scotland+-+opinion/&threadPage=1 .

6

talking and living, as has become popular from about the '60s onwards.[15] As such, postmodern talk came to serve as a philosophical justification for the relativism around. It also muddied the waters sufficiently to make regulative ideals such as truth, knowledge and evidence for (or against) a claim, seem hopeless endeavours. We return to this in the next chapter.

All this and more presses institutions for change and transformation, with one clear consequence being the question about *differences*. That is to say, how to deal fairly, equitably, and justly with differences – individual differences; religious, linguistic, and other cultural differences; gender and sexual-choice differences; class differences, and more – is radically uncertain. This has become an even more pressing problem since 9/11, the 'War on Terror,' and related world-wide challenges to power.

We have thus a global situation characterised by more rather than less attention to differences, and a greater emphasis on advocating tolerance,[16] and 'the ability not to be overly disconcerted by differences from oneself, not to respond aggressively to such differences'[17] – obviously within certain limits.[18] At the same time, schooling (excluding elite sites of education[19]), increasingly suffers under values, commitments and projects that are nonetheless worthy of our social and political consideration: equality, tolerance for differences, contested authorities and traditions, and pluralism.

All in all, we have considerable support for (cultural) relativism in our judgements, and various explicit avowals of the value of diversity[20] and

---

[15] Toulmin, *Cosmopolis.*
[16] Rorty, R., *Truth and Progress. Philosophical Papers* (Cambridge: CUP, 1998), 186–201.
[17] *Ibid.*, 186.
[18] Comte-Sponville, A., *A Short Treatise on the Great Virtues. The Uses of Philosophy in Everyday Life* (London: Vintage, 2003), 157–72.
[19] Elite forms of education keep difference to a minimum; cf.
http://www.questia.com/search/cultural-history-education ; and
http://www.questia.com/PM.qst?a=o&d=54447684 . Nonetheless, I am *not* concerned with elite schools or those who are able to afford special schooling.
[20] Goodhart, 'Too diverse?', 30.

multiculturalism.[21] My problem is that when these are used to frame what is taught or included in the curriculum of formal, mass education, things become more rather than less difficult. For example, the inculcation of strong commitments, as well as certain evaluations and identifications, seems to me to require something other from teachers than that they are qualified in one or other domain of *knowledge*: they have to share these commitments, or be morally or politically convinced by them, in order to transmit them sincerely.

We are also compelled to acknowledge that secular, modern societies no longer abide by one clear vision about the good (or end) for 'man' (the individual human being universalised, neutralised and neutered, as critics would say of this older term). It is almost impossible, nowadays, unlike it was for Aristotle (384–322 BC), to defend one function or defining activity for man *qua* man, to suggest that happiness lies in the good performance of this activity (reasoning), and to conclude, from this, that the good life for man is the life in which reasoning is maintained.[22] I am however not inclined, like Alasdair MacIntyre,[23] to call us back to a self-understanding for which social conditions may no longer exist, in order to improve on education in the present case – even though I find much to agree with in his account of a life worth living.[24]

Duly recognising the cultures of others,[25] and promoting mutual understanding, tolerance, and ways in which one culture could be prevented from dominating others – or practising what Haack calls 'social multiculturalism' – is

---

[21] Haack, S., *Manifesto of a Passionate Moderate* (Chicago: University of Chicago Press, 1998), 137–48.
[22] Cf. Aristotle, *The Nicomachean Ethics of Aristotle*, (Intro. by J.A. Smith), trans. D.P. Chase (London: J.M. Dent and Sons Ltd, 1949); Aristotle, *The Politics of Aristotle*, trans. with notes by E. Barker (Oxford: The Clarendon Press, 1948); and Aristotle, *A Treatise on Government*, trans. W. Ellis (London: J.M. Dent and Sons Ltd, 1941).
[23] MacIntyre, A., *After Virtue. A Study in Moral Theory* (London: Duckworth, 1992).
[24] As I argue elsewhere; Craig, A.P., *What is the Self? A Philosophy of Psychology* (Lewiston: The Edwin Mellen Press, Ltd, 2006).
[25] I am usually wary of this word 'culture' because it is used to mean, imply, and refer to too much; cf. Craig, A.P., 'Culture and the individual', *Theory and Psychology*, 13/5 (2003), 629–50. I use it to mean quite simply *shared habits of action* and do not include strong evaluations as a definitive part of these habits.

clearly a good thing; and so is endorsing what she calls 'pluralistic educational multiculturalism' or 'the idea that it is desirable for students to know about other cultures than their own'.[26] The trouble starts with relativism about *knowledge*. A useful approach to this is Isaiah Berlin's[27] distinctions between 'pluralism' and 'relativism' (he reserves the latter term for doubts about objective knowledge, the possibility of objective, neutral evidence for factual claims), and relativism and 'historicism'.

About pluralism, Berlin notes how Vico's historicism[28] entailed the difficult task of trying to understand or enter the world of others through the ultimate values and ends that they pursued.

> We are urged to look upon life as affording a plurality of values, equally genuine, equally ultimate, above all equally objective; incapable, therefore, of being ordered in a timeless hierarchy, or judged in terms of some one absolute standard.[29]

And on relativism Berlin writes:

> There are at least two types of relativism, that of judgements of fact, and that of judgements of values. The first, in its strongest form, denies the very possibility of objective knowledge of facts, since all belief is conditioned by the place in the social system, and therefore by the interests, conscious or not, of the theorists, or of the group or class to which they belong. The weaker version ... exempts the natural sciences from this predicament, or identifies a privileged group ... as being, somewhat mysteriously, free from these distorting factors.[30]

'Historicism,' for Berlin, has to do with Vico and Herder's insistence that 'human thought and action are fully intelligible only in relation to their historical

---

[26] Haack, *Manifesto of a Passionate Moderate*, 137.

[27] Berlin, I., *The Crooked Timber of Humanity* (New York: Vintage Books, 1992).

[28] See Berlin's discussion of Vico and Herder, in Berlin, I., *Against the Current. Essays in the History of Ideas* (Intro. by R. Hausheer), Hardy, H. (ed.) (Oxford: OUP, 1981), 111–29; and Berlin, I., *The Roots of Romanticism* (The A.W. Mellon Lectures in the Fine Arts. The National Gallery of Art, Washington DC, Bollingen Series xxxv, 45), Hardy, H. (ed.) (Princeton, NJ: Princeton University Press, 1999).

[29] *Ibid.*, 79.

[30] *Ibid.*, 74.

context'[31] (a position also argued for by Wittgenstein and Peter Winch[32]); whereas relativism about matters of fact is, for Berlin, ultimately an incoherent position.

I agree with Berlin and think it crucial to separate debates about certainty or securing *facts* through good, strong supporting evidence,[33] from the plurality of *values* in terms of which people direct their lives and judge self and others. Furthermore, it is important to distinguish between, on the one hand, the manner in which our grasp of the *history* of a people or their ideas facilitates our ability to understand their beliefs and actions (even though this does not commit us to agreement with their choices, values and so forth) and, on the other, *knowledge* of this or that event, action and so on. It is typically our historicity and values (or commitments, identifications and strong evaluations) that furnish us with background beliefs, or those beliefs we do not question.

The particular point that I want to underline is that running together these difficulties and complexities about different values and histories, in addition to confusing pluralism, relativism and historicism about values and knowledge, makes for very poor approaches to education. Moreover, that there are difficulties associated with separating different values and beliefs-in-context (background beliefs) from objective evidence or the facts of a matter does not relegate the hope for reasonable discussion or rational discourse to the rubbish heap of the past. I thus do not credit epistemic relativism with much more than frightening us with the thought that *difficulties* with separating background beliefs from neutral evidence are insurmountable and as such with ruling out the possibility of justified true beliefs or knowledge.[34] More about this in Chapter 2.

The way in which relativism creeps into education and undermines its

---

[31] *Ibid.*, 77.
[32] Cf. Cioffi, F., *Wittgenstein on Freud and Frazer* (Cambridge: CUP, 1998); and Winch, P., *The Idea of a Social Science* (London: Routledge and Kegan Paul, 1970).
[33] Haack, S., *Evidence and Inquiry. Towards Reconstruction in Epistemology* (Oxford: Blackwell, 1995).
[34] Cf. Haack, *Evidence and Inquiry*; Haack, *Manifesto of a Passionate Moderate*, 149–66, and 188–208; and Koertge, N. (ed.), *A House Built on Sand. Exposing Postmodernist Myths about Science* (Oxford: OUP, 2000).

focus is, however, worth emphasising by way of getting rid of it. Emphasising *relevance* rather than epistemic criteria as a way of assessing the worth of knowledge is more about making a political point about power and about an assumed relationship between power and knowledge which, it is further assumed, is not open to the test of evidence for or against the claim to knowledge.[35] The emphasis on relevance is a political project often phrased in terms of postmodern and anti-science talk,[36] and often couched in terms reminiscent of the dreams and ideologies of the '60s, or the leftover sentiments from this era.[37] I have come to consider these moves tedious, at best, and destructive of education's noblest hopes, at worst.[38]

Having said all that, I would still want to support tolerance for differences; such tolerance grows from an appreciation of the plurality of values pursued by different societies at various times. In addition, we have to acknowledge the impact on us of the fact that our thoughts and actions are deeply embedded in a context, and thus open to the influence of history, language, and so on. This too, however, requires some critical comment. The pervasive relativism that characterises western societies sponsors both a refusal to take a stand and an inability or lameness in the face of values, ends, and strong evaluations that deserve to be questioned and rejected. Wishy-washy tolerance is hardly a way to prepare those whom 'the Greeks simply called ... the new ones'[39] for a world that

---

[35] Haack, *Manifesto of a Passionate Moderate*, undertakes a systematic review of the various issues involved in what she terms 'a great revolutionary chorus of voices announcing that disinterested inquiry is impossible, that all supposed "knowledge" is an expression of power, that the concepts of evidence, objectivity, truth, are ideological humbug' (ix). There is little in this work that I do not agree with.

[36] Cf. Bernstein, R.J., *Beyond Objectivism and Relativism* (Oxford: Blackwell, 1983); and Koertge, *A House Built on Sand*.

[37] Rejection of the words and works, and especially the power, of 'dead, white European males'. See Bloom for his rejection, in turn, of those he groups together as 'the School of Resentment' (Feminists, Afrocentrists, Marxists, Foucault-inspired New Historicists, or Deconstructors); Bloom, H., *The Western Canon* (London: Papermac, 1995), 20, 39.

[38] Cf. Hoggart, R., *The Way We Live Now* (London: Chatto and Windus, 1995).

[39] Arendt, H., *Between Past and Future* (London: Penguin, 1993), 176.

they will at best change for the better.[40] The difficult issue about all this has to do with what belongs at home and what belongs to the classroom.[41]

We are increasingly living in ways that relegate more of what used to be the provenance of the home to the classroom (e.g. sex education, moral teaching, exposure to specific role models, say, in the form of gay teachers). This shift, again, demands an appreciation of the sensitivities of different 'others'. My issue is with the inroads this makes into schooling's focus on delivering a numerate, literate, and educated society. Limited resources and the question of how to deal fairly with conflicting values, identities, etc. in *shared* sites of exchange, compel us to ask what a specific focus on these differences demands of teachers and teaching.

I thus want to acknowledge a changed situation and ask about the influence of this on mass education. As regards the situation the world is in, I believe that porous state boundaries (open to the movement of people, ideas, money, and force/violence) and real-time contacts between people and organisations separated by vast distances, impose new constraints on education (and on life, in general, and politics and self-understanding, in particular).[42] These are constraints that, coupled with mass education, really make the picture look very different to me.

For one thing, controlling the code or mastering and having access to available technology and knowledge really *can* liberate someone from a physical placement or specific locale like never before, which also means, of course, that universal standardisation is equally in the face or on the desk of both the most geographically isolated and the most centrally located person. For another, it is also possible to share a symbolic universe with very distant and even unknown others, like never before. That is to say, there are enough virtual contacts and

[40] I am going over this part of the text as the news of the bombs on the London Tube and a double-decker bus (2005/07/07) are coming over the airwaves – yet another reminder that all is not well; that neither wishy-washy tolerance nor sowing terror is good enough for improving things.
[41] See Rosin, H., 'God and country', *The New Yorker* (27 June 2003), 44–9, for a discussion of one remarkable trend in the homeschooling movement and beyond.
[42] Cf. Giddens, *The Consequences of Modernity*.

networks to keep most idiosyncratic, esoteric, and even secret, interests, commitments and identifications going through the World Wide Web (www), so that fewer and fewer nowadays have to depend only on what is available in face-to-face situations to maintain their particular interests. But, choosing this way of communicating (even in order to keep globalising tendencies at bay) comes at a price – the price of maintaining a universalising code.

I therefore want to separate state-funded schooling from whatever *additional* schooling, training, or inculcation of religious, ideological, or cultural values any particular group wants or requires for their young, or demands in the name of their own group's survival amidst universalising/globalising/westernising influences. How far everybody's tax should go to fund particularistic requirements is thus an issue I do not address, but it is obviously one that motivates debates about solidarity versus diversity,[43] immigration policies, and the integration of minorities (immigrant, refugee, and other newcomers) into various schooling systems.[44] As far as public schooling goes, the issue for me has to do with available resources, including the expertise of teachers, and the time devoted to particularistic needs and multicultural socialisation versus what I want to suggest is the heart of schooling.

It thus seems to me utterly unwise and economically indefensible to spend any time or resources on the inculcation of particularistic religious, ideological, or cultural values when this occurs at the cost of teaching learners what they need to know and do in order to be successful in a globalised world. I think that a focus on 'universal standardisation' will invigorate mass schooling; and I believe, too, that this is yet again a way to underline the recurring need[45] to attend to what will undercut the wars of differences raging everywhere. This time, though, I do not

---

[43] Cf. Goodhart, 'Too diverse?'.
[44] Cf. Craig, A.P. and Beishuizen, J.J., 'Psychological testing in a multicultural society: Universal or particular competencies', *Intercultural Education*, 13/2 (2002), 201–13.
[45] 'Again' in the sense that Reason, Science, the Utopian visions of the 20th century, and more, have been attempts to impose such agreement before; Toulmin speculates how much the death of Henry of Navarre might have later influenced Descartes's own attempt to find a single certain thing on which to build other certainties (*Cosmopolis*, 62).

intend any metaphysical, political, or theoretical vision, but merely want to underline a *de facto* situation – one that education must attend to.

With 'universal standardisation' I mean, negatively put, the manner in which technology tends *not* to respect individual idiosyncrasies, cultural particularities and other non-standard requirements when it fills the world with gadgets from the mundane (e.g. bottle openers), to the once exotic but now fast becoming ordinary in certain quarters (e.g. Global Positioning Devices such as an in-vehicle navigation system)[46] – albeit that such gadgets allow for the tracking of highly personal and specific goals and needs!

The conditions of most lives, in a globalised world, are such that individuals and communities *may* participate in what is available and on offer, albeit only to the degree that they *can* do so. This highlights both the fact of increasing universal standardisation – from the ubiquitous mobile phone to information and knowledge on the www – and the importance of controlling such codes in order to participate in what is on offer. The skills and knowledge that we require to operate available technology are therefore much more than what we are all naturally equipped with, in terms of simply having an opposable thumb or a specific hand-eye-brain configuration, but also depend on our being able to extend our human (cognitive abilities) by knowing how to use what is between people (symbols, signs, language, knowledge, tools and technology) to achieve more than what we could achieve as isolated individuals.

Positively, therefore, universally standardised skills, technology and knowledge refer to those *human* accomplishments that provide the positioning, support, or scaffolding 'in which human reason is able to far outstrip the computational ambit of the unaugmented brain'. 'Advanced reason' (Andy Clark tells us) 'is ... above all the realm of the *scaffolded* brain: the brain in its bodily

---

[46] Cf. http://www.gpsworld.com/gpsworld/ .

context, interacting with a complex world of physical and social structures'.[47] But before the world outside 'skin and skull'[48] can be or become available to us, we must learn to exercise *control over the code.*

Controlling the code starts from the basic, and I almost want to say 'original', *skills* taught in schools, i.e. the 3Rs, and goes on to those natural languages with a world-wide reach (e.g. English, Spanish), non-natural languages (e.g. mathematics, software codes), knowledge that explains what makes the world go round[49] (e.g. natural science, biology), and knowledge that locates us in a cosmos (e.g. history, geography). I do not mean to indicate some mini-curriculum, only to underline that which anyone, anywhere, would recognise as part of global, intellectual currency.

Technology goes back into the evolutionary past of ourselves and our near-animal relatives.[50] Nowadays, technology is more closely informed by scientific knowledge, which is more recent,[51] but even before this our manipulative skills as 'natural-born cyborgs'[52] underwrote technological innovation and the quest for knowledge. The enormous influence of scientific knowledge on our lives also means that the skills and knowledge needed to use available technology involve us daily in more than technological standardisation.

Knowledge, or justified true belief, implies an appreciation of *evidence* for or against a theory/claim, knowing how to draw *logical* inferences, and understanding how to use other sound thinking skills, which are indeed *human* cognitive capacities. The ability to assess evidence and related matters is also the

---

[47] Clark, A., *Being There. Putting Brain, Body, and World Together Again* (Cambridge, MA: The MIT Press, 1999), 191.

[48] Clark, A., 'Reasons, robots and the extended mind', *Mind and Language*, 16/2 (2001), 138.

[49] Even the most convinced religious zealot can and still does use the internet, universal chemistry, etc. to fashion his tools of destruction – albeit in the name of some very unique, particularistic vision.

[50] Cf. Tattersall, I., 'Once we were not alone', *Scientific American* (25 August 2003), 20–27.

[51] Cf. Wolpert, L., *The Unnatural Nature of Science* (Cambridge, MA: Harvard University Press, 1997).

[52] Clark, A., *Natural-born Cyborgs. Minds, Technologies, and the Future of Human Intelligence* (Oxford: OUP, 2003); and Clark, A., 'Where brain, body, and world collide', *Cognitive Systems Research*, 1/1 (1999), 5–17.

tool with which to engage and distinguish *knowledge* from, say, mere opinion, anywhere.[53] This, coupled with knowing where to find the best of current knowledge or information on an issue, will go a long way towards equipping the user with the wherewithal to enter global exchanges.

Moreover, that knowledge, like science and mathematics, is generally understood in *universal* terms, rather than in terms of specific indigenous achievements, is noteworthy. Gardner writes, for example: 'A Chinese mathematician is no more concerned with ancient Chinese mathematics, remarkable though it was, than a Western physicist is concerned with the physics of Aristotle.'[54] For the rest – the much loved home languages, specific religions, dearly held cultural rituals and beliefs, and so forth – I think that each group must find the place and means to express and continue these to the benefit of themselves, their identities, and the richness of the total stock of human goods; not, however, in shared sites of exchange, open and even compulsory to all.

A question we are left with at this point has to do with the spread of various basic technologies (from writing to print to computer and other electronic means of communication) on a global scale. Phrased differently: what about the fact that the world is *already* divided between those who have and those who do not have access to, control over, and the means to utilise available technology and knowledge? My answer, inasmuch as it goes towards solving this massive problem, is that providing the have-nots with particularistic education (perhaps in an attempt to minimise their felt disadvantage?), or culturally valued skills, hardly suffices to equip them with the means to transcend their impoverished situation. The solution thus lies in solving the problem (poorly distributed resources) and not in plastering this over with cheap talk about valuing the knowledge of the local medicine man as highly as that of the nuclear scientist, or the knowledge of cows' faces and individual colours as highly as the knowledge of mathematics.

[53] Cf. Kuhn, D., 'Science as argument: Implications for teaching and learning scientific thinking', *Science Education*, 77/3 (1993), 319–37.
[54] Gardner, 'The New New Math'.

16

A difficult issue regarding my proposal for a focus on universally standardised skills, technology and knowledge has to do with what I will address in Chapter 5: the *history* of tasks. Suffice it here to flag this difficulty as a clash between the skills and technology, and cognition and knowledge valued or familiar in one culture, and those demanded by the tasks of a new or alien culture. It is not often acknowledged that all tasks, including those that define parenting, or are included in a school curriculum (e.g. ongoing question-answer exchanges between child and parent, the 3Rs, psychometric tests, independent study) are part and parcel of a certain group's history of fitting into, and having made its home over time in, a particular place.

When the history of tasks is acknowledged, it is usually done in the sense of wanting to excuse a particular group's inability to perform on certain tasks, or to criticise the imposition of one form (e.g. western logic) on contexts where this is an alien manner of operating on tasks.[55] This helps no one. When immigration, colonisation, or other mass upheavals and movements force whole groups into an alien culture's institutions, the hidden processes of education come very clearly to the fore, as it also places a special burden on those involved in education.

1.2 Three stories about education

Frankena, in the *Dictionary of the History of Ideas*,[56] clarifies the enterprise of education as follows:

> [It] consists in all forms and places of activity in which some individual or group fosters or seeks to foster in some individual or group some ability, belief, knowledge, habit, skill, trait of character, or 'value', and does so by the use of certain methods. There is always someone doing the educating, someone being educated, something being fostered in the second by the first, by some method or combination of methods.[57]

---

[55] Cf. Luria, A.R., *Cognitive Development. Its Cultural and Social Foundations* (Cambridge, MA: Harvard University Press, 1976); and Ogbu, J.U., 'Origins of human competence: A cultural-ecological perspective', *Child Development*, 52 (1981), 413–29.
[56] Cf. http://etext.lib.virginia.edu/cgi-local/DHI/dhi.cgi?id=dv2-08 .
[57] *Idem.*

This general description does not get us far, but it does get us going; we note, for example, three different *kinds* of foci: (1) belief and knowledge; (2) ability, habit, skill, and (3) traits of character and value. In my view, it is the last of these that has no place as an explicit focus in mass or universal schooling for reasons outlined above. I concluded that focusing on universally standardised skills, technology and knowledge will make mass schooling *possible, relevant,* and *efficient.*[58] What should be left out of schooling in my view is character-building as a specific focus (which is not to say that this will not happen, by and by, during the process of someone acquiring mastery over the code), and the inculcation of other particularistic habits, traits, values and ideological commitments. This, of course, does not mean that extra-school, private, or additional teaching, still in some way part of the overall project of 'education', as Frankena describes it, is not possible or even desirable to some.

Frankena suggests, furthermore, that:

> ... we can and do think of education in different but related ways: (1) as the activity of the one doing the educating, the act or process of *educating* or *teaching* engaged in by the educator, (2) as the process or experience of *being educated* or *learning* that goes on in the one being educated, and (3) as the *result* produced in the one being educated by the double process of educating and being educated, i.e., the combination of abilities, etc., that are produced in him or that are possessed by him when he has been educated. In these three uses of 'education' we are referring to the enterprise of education in one way or another, but we also think of education in a fourth way, namely, (4) as the discipline or study [once called 'pedagogics', often set up as a department or school within a college or university, and thought of as subject matter to be taught and developed by further research].[59]

In light of the above, my concern in this book is with points (3) and (4) in the quotation above; that is to say, with *what is produced in the one being educated* (control over the code), and with the study of cognition as that discipline through which subject experts are turned into teachers.

---

[58] Cf. Friedman, T. *The World is Flat: A Brief History of the Twenty-first Century* (New York: Farrar, Strauss and Giroux, 2005).
[59] Frankena, http://etext.lib.virginia.edu/cgi-local/DHI/dhi.cgi?id=dv2-08 . The emphasis and bracketed explanations are also Frankena's.

18

Lastly, and by way of introducing the next story about education, we note the four outstanding revolutions in educational theory of modern times listed by Frankena: the movement towards *child-centredness*, the rise of *secularism*, the introduction of *science and other modern subjects* into the curriculum, and a belief in *universal education* (part compulsory, free and public). I now turn to Hannah Arendt's still-relevant ideas on what is wrong with education.[60]

For Arendt, what is wrong with education during 'The Century of the Child'[61] has to do with three factors: (a) forgetting that childhood is temporary and thus thinking of the child's world as autonomous, and governable by children; (b) separating *what* is taught from *how* it is taught, or undermining knowledge of the subject matter though a focus on pedagogy; and (c) a view of learning as conducted according to the belief 'that you can know and understand only what you have done yourself'.[62] As regards the first, she notes the basic or natural asymmetry between parent and child, and teacher and pupil; an asymmetry that emphasises the degree to which the child is at the mercy of and dependent on the ministrations of first one and then the other for life, learning, and entering the world through schooling. Arendt considers the basic asymmetry 'natural' in the sense of it being a basic condition of our lives, of our 'natality, the fact that human beings are born into the world'.[63] Arendt locates the teacher's specific authority in subject-specific expertise; so that to conceive of teaching in terms *other* than this is, for her, to create a breakdown in learning-teaching. Her last point (against a fashionable conception of learning-as-doing) is also worth noting.

I am in agreement with Arendt on the responsibility of teachers and parents in view of the nature of childhood, and that learning entails much more than doing (her points a and c), but my agreement with (b) – separating *what* is taught from *how* it is taught – is qualified. Suffice it to point in this regard to the

---

[60] Arendt, *Between Past and Future*, 173–96.
[61] *Ibid.*, 187.
[62] *Ibid.*, 180–5.
[63] *Ibid.*, 174.

demands of mass schooling, i.e. in multicultural contexts of exchange; a more or less global situation that also attenuates what we could mean by a focus in schooling on the old world into which each new generation is born, as I discuss below. Both my agreement and disagreement are further discussed in the following chapters.

What is worth noting here is that Arendt's account makes us see both the necessarily ordinariness of schooling (e.g. a focus on the 3Rs), and something grander. What is grander has to do with the role schooling plays in the crucial mediation between our natural condition as *living* creatures, on the one hand, and our striving as *human* participants and agents in a world, on the other.

Arendt's tantalising piece on the interaction between the old and the new, conservation and innovation, education and politics is worth quoting at length:

> ... it seems to me that conservatism, in the sense of conservation, is of the essence of the educational activity, whose task is always to cherish and protect something – the child against the world, the world against the child, the new against the old, the old against the new. Even the comprehensive responsibility for the world that is thereby assumed, implies, of course, a conservative attitude. But this holds good only for the realm of education, or rather for the relations between grown-ups and children, and not for the realm of politics, where we act among and with adults and equals. In politics this conservative attitude – which accepts the world as it is, striving only to preserve the status quo – can only lead to destruction, because the world, in gross and in detail, is irrevocably delivered up to the ruin of time unless human beings are determined to intervene, to alter, to create what is new ... Our hope always hangs on the new which every generation brings; but precisely because we can base our hope only on this, we destroy everything if we so try to control the new that we, the old, can dictate how it will look. Exactly for the sake of what is new and revolutionary in every child, education must be conservative; it must preserve this newness and introduce it as a new thing into an old world, which, however revolutionary its actions may be, is always, from the standpoint of the next generation, superannuated and close to destruction.[64]

I think the above salutary advice when neither politics (on a global scale) nor education, in many countries, is delivering the goods, and when education is

---

[64] Arendt, *Between Past and Future*, 192–3.

politicised perhaps specifically because it is the *young* who feel compelled to set things right.[65] Further, many bemoan the quality of the product at the end of years of schooling as well as the methods and aims of education,[66] and too many *grown-ups* have withdrawn from voting in elections and thus from exercising their right and duty to change things politically. Arendt emphasises therefore that the task of those involved in educating the new ones is to allow them to grow into an *old* world; that, in fact, if they are prepared for a *new* world, they are robbed of their own intent on renewal. In her words,

> It is in the very nature of the human condition that each new generation grows into an old world, so that to prepare a new generation for a new world can only mean that one wishes to strike from the newcomers' hands their own chance at the new.[67]

During revolutionary upheavals of what was/is, or in preparation for a new Utopia (e.g. the state-orchestrated experiments of the 20th century), great pains are taken, of course, to prepare everybody (including the new ones) for a *new* world. And it is partly in resistance to this, and partly in view of her ideas about childhood and the roles of parents and teachers, that Arendt draws the distinctions she does between the *old* world and the *new* human beings born into it. They are new in the sense that they are still to become fully *human*, which makes the child in this regard different from other living things with whom the child nonetheless shares the process of becoming, as such. This double aspect of the life of the child, indicating a relationship to the *world* on the one hand, and to *life* on the other, is what gives education its uniquely *human* face according to Arendt.

The old world into which children are born requires some discussion if we are not to overburden present learning with the past. I would say that if too much of the past is taken on as being valuably 'old', education becomes impossible – especially in the clamour, as outlined above, for equal recognition of differences,

---

[65] Cf. Hamlet's words, 'The time is out of joint. O cursed spite that ever I was born to set it right', quoted in Arendt, *Between Past and Future*, 192.
[66] Cf. Hoggart, *The Way We Live Now*.
[67] *Ibid.*, 177.

conflicting commitments, and so on. The world into which children are born is thus old in the sense that certain modes of living, knowing and coping exist in it as a matter of fact. The *de facto* situation thus sets certain goals, standards, or aims for education. The task, then, for parents and teachers, is to equip the young with the wherewithal to succeed in *this* world, *as it is*, and perhaps in the hope that once the young ones control the code they will do better than those before them.

What seems to me to have gone wrong since the '60s is the old ones' insistence on shaping the schools, and any other institution they could reach, for a future *they* wanted; but this is indeed to strike the opportunity for renewal from the newcomers' hands, as Arendt argues. And I am suggesting, that what Bloom calls 'the School of Resentment' (Feminists, Afrocentrists, Marxists, Foucault-inspired New Historicists, or Deconstructors), certainly has a hand in this insistence. The point is: too much relativism, multiculturalism and other 'isms' might just be bad for schooling (and probably parenting too). What lends some support to this argument is the fact that schooling fails most spectacularly when it attempts to be original and radical, for example, in deschooling,[68] Fuzzy Math,[69]

---

[68] Cf. http://www.ecotopia.com/webpress/deschooling.htm and http://www.deschooling.org/ .

[69] Cf. Gardner, 'The New New Math', 248. I quote from this at length: 'In the late 1960s the National Council of Teachers of Mathematics (NCTM) began to promote a reform movement called the New Math. In an effort to give students insight into why arithmetic works, it placed a heavy emphasis on set theory, congruence arithmetic, and the use of number bases other than ten. Children were forbidden to call, say, 7 a "number". It was a "numeral" that symbolized a number. The result was enormous confusion on the part of pupils, teachers, and parents. The New Math fad faded after strong attacks by the physicist Richard Feynman and others. The final blow was administered by the mathematician Morris Kline's 1973 best seller *Why Johnny Can't Add: The Failure of the New Math*. ... Recently, the NCTM, having learned little from its New Math fiasco, has once more been backing another reform movement that goes by such names as the new new math, whole math, fuzzy math, standards math, and rain forest math. Like the old New Math, it is creating a ferment among teachers and parents, especially in California, where it first caught on. It is estimated that about half of all pre-college mathematics in the United States is now being taught by teachers trained in fuzzy math. The new fad is heavily influenced by multiculturalism, environmentalism, and feminism. These trends get much attention in the twenty-eight papers contributed to the NCTM's 1997 yearbook, *Multicultural and Gender Equity in the Mathematics Classroom: The Gift of Diversity* ... Fuzzy-math teachers are urged by contributors to the yearbook to cut down on lecturing to passive listeners. No longer are they to play the role of "sage on stage". They are the "guide on the side". Classes are divided into small groups of students who cooperate in finding solutions to "open-ended" problems by trial and error. This is called "interactive learning". The use of calculators is encouraged, along with such visual aids as

22

and 'Reading-for-Meaning' or 'whole-language learning'.[70]

My own ideas about education were born in the crucible of apartheid South Africa – a place well-known enough for the struggles against apartheid, the eventual release of Nelson Mandela (1990), and the first non-racial elections (1994) – to cut a long story short. It is a story that is neither original nor grand,[71] and that has a basic theme: the distribution of power and privilege. This abbreviated statement of the network of control over sources of power, the conflicting identities and cultural self-understanding, and the local, regional, national and international goals and strategies, all of which underwrote the South African version of exploitation, oppression, and the violation of human rights, obviously leaves a great deal unsaid.

I do not intend to go into the particular, South African brand of 'man's inhumanity to man'; suffice it to underline the extent to which this also influenced and still influences education. It was during the dying days of apartheid South Africa (1986–91) that I came to develop a particular view on education; before

---

counters, geometrical models, geoboards, wax paper (for folding conic section curves), tiles of different colors and shapes, and other devices. Getting a correct answer is considered less important than shrewd guesses based on insights, hence the term "fuzzy math". Formal proofs are downgraded.'

[70] Cf. http://www.lblp.com/downloads/PDF/research/Gestalt.pdf .

[71] Without wanting to discount or diminish the suffering of particular individuals, the various ways in which people were made to feel inferior in the country of their birth, and the deliberate blocks to change and development of indigenous cultures as well as their integration into other forms of life, I regard the 50 years or so under the set of official discriminatory laws known as 'apartheid' as small fry in terms of the world's evils or 'man's inhumanity to man'. It is nonetheless a story that inspired and moved people far removed from South Africa to one or the other form of 'anti-apartheid' politics, albeit often of the token kind, and called forth greater interest than concurrent situations of seemingly greater evil. In addition, I mean by 'not original' that the exploitation of indigenous groups by conquering settlers is not new in the history of the settling of territories; and by 'not grand' that it was petty, mean and shameful in intent and form, rather than being of a kind that could, in retrospect, make one gasp at the scale of human evil (e.g. such as the deliberate extermination of Jews during World War II). I would thus argue that the costs of apartheid slipped through the Truth and Reconciliation Commission's hands (because it wanted to capture something original and grand about the past to justify its own quasi-religious platform and approach), and that the hardest part of calculating the cost has to do with measuring what it has meant, and still does, to have been thought unworthy of human dignity, responsibility and duty; a way of thinking that also has a tendency to become internalised (cf. Paulo Freire's 'Pedagogy of the Oppressed', http://www-distance.syr.edu/pvitapf.html , also http://www.paulofreire.org/), and thus over-powering and self-perpetuating.

this, education (either as an institution or as a label for the collection of activities housed in schools, departments or faculties at universities, or teacher training colleges) was not a concern of mine. What drew me in was and is an abiding interest: cognition or, more accurately, 'applied cognition'.

After participating in a series of Vygotskian-inspired studies during the early part of the '80s, I approached (in 1986) an executive member of the University of Natal, Durban Campus (now called the University of KwaZulu-Natal), who was charged with the task of overseeing what was then called Student Support Services, to offer my services. Student Support Services was to develop under him into a more wide-ranging academic development initiative.

The pervasive idea then was that the high failure rate among black students in South Africa had something to do with language difficulties; and thus supporting students with their university studies, in particular, involved mostly additional (English) language teaching. I had different ideas: briefly, that apartheid exploited, maintained, and deepened *differences* between, what I want to call here for the sake of brevity, 'western forms' (of thinking, doing, and knowledge) and 'African forms'. This meant, educationally speaking, that black, African students were confronted with university tasks that were both *cognitively* unfamiliar (and in this they were in the same boat as all new students), and (often) *culturally* unfamiliar. This meant that black African students confronted a double load, or entered and engaged university studies handicapped, as it were. It thus seemed to me that the task of educational support must involve *decoding the unfamiliarity of the tasks* for students so as to facilitate successful and independent engagement. These ideas were motivated by my own doctoral research, which involved the study of Zulu-speaking mother-child and teacher-child interaction.[72]

---

[72] Craig, A.P., 'On the method of analysing human transactions recorded on videotape', *South African Journal of Psychology*, 18/3 (1988), 96–103; and Craig, A.P., *Mothers and Children: An Analysis of Change* (Unpublished doctoral dissertation, Department of Psychology, University of Natal, Durban, 1985). When this doctoral work was nearing completion (1984), I presented

From 1986 to 1988 I pursued two questions regarding a range of university tasks empirically: (1) what are the cognitive demands of the tasks; and (2) what do students need to *know* and *do* in order to succeed with university studies? This involved mining for and reconstructing the taken-for-granted and implicit, but nonetheless definitive 'rules of the game' and 'tricks of the trade' underlying university studies (as some kind of a whole), as well as particular tasks, courses, or disciplines. I worked on a variety of materials, obtained from senior lecturers/professors in disciplines across the arts and humanities, and social sciences, and later, with the assistance of postgraduate students, in anatomy and mathematics.[73] The materials consisted of lecture notes, video recordings of lectures given, student essays and exam scripts, and a few interviews with students. I argued that once explicated these rules and tricks could be turned into teaching and learning foci – together with the appropriate substantial content.

At the end of 1988 we[74] used this empirical background as the basis for what we called the Teach-Test-Teach (TTT) programme, which ran as a pilot for three years. TTT was a programme that changed from year to year on the basis of the data gathered and analysed after each intake of students; data on the extent to which the programme actually bridged the gap between what the students brought to the learning-teaching situation (their habitual responses or existing knowledge

videotapes of the 'work in progress' on mother-child and teacher-child instructional transactions on a task designed by James Wertsch to a postgraduate seminar group of his at Northwestern University (USA). After my return to South Africa, Wertsch wrote to my supervisor (R. Miller) to break off all further contact with us on account of the academic boycott and pressure from his students after my seminar there. This effectively isolated interesting Vygotskian work done at University of Natal, Durban Campus, for the duration of the boycott.

[73] Craig, A.P. and Winter, P.A., 'The meta- and epistemic constraints on praxis: The learning-teaching dialectic in mathematics', *Perspectives in Education*, 13/1 (1991–2), 45–67; also Craig, A.P. and Kernoff, R.J., 'An analysis of underprepared students' developing textual interpretation', *South African Journal of Higher Education*, 9/1 (1995), 23–30; Craig, A.P. and Bradbury, J.L., *A Guide to Learning* (Kenwyn: Juta and Co. Ltd, 1994); Craig, A.P., Griesel, H. and Witz. L., *Conceptual Dictionary* (Kenwyn: Juta and Co. Ltd, 1994); Craig, A.P. and Winter, P.A., 'An analysis of learners' engagement in mathematical tasks', *South African Journal of Higher Education*, 4/1 (1990), 59–68; and Craig, A.P., *The Production of Knowledge* (Durban: Tegwen Publications; TTT Publications, 1988 [1989 revised]).

[74] Note that from the first intake of students, at the end of 1988, 'I' turns into 'we' – what I have to say however involves only my own thinking from the start.

and skills), and what the tasks demanded, as well as how selected students actually managed their university studies. It is worth noting that this work had a considerable influence on others working on similar problems at other South African universities.

In view of fears about universalising discourses, it is good to note too that whatever *was* achieved through TTT, the one thing this programme utterly failed in was to turn the students who were successfully educated into blind followers, or indoctrinated subjects, of any of the systems or ideologies of which my colleagues and I were supporters or unwitting parts.

Once people know, and know what to do to succeed, they know well enough to choose for themselves how to live and who to be. The most splendid achievement of any education/educator is to equip learners with the skills and knowledge they need in order to succeed, and if this includes equipping them with the wherewithal to change the world into a better place, so much the better.

Questions about learning and teaching, from my first forays into education, have always lacked the ease with which one may engage intellectual pursuits without political roots and clear practical costs. But even though my views on learning and teaching were shaped by apartheid South Africa, I do not think that what I have to say only applies to this or similar situations. It is, however, frequently the case that in multicultural settings, outside abundant resources, problems in thinking about learning and teaching are more starkly exposed.

The argument motivating the book as a whole could now be summarised as follows: in the above, I outlined some of the problems that beset education; problems that I believe will be addressed if the focus of schooling were to shift to universally standardised skills, technology and knowledge. Such a shift will demand of teachers[75] both expertise in their teaching-discipline, and some grasp of the issues involved in knowing, learning, perceiving, thinking and so on, in short, of 'cognition'. But, given my diagnosis of the ills that beset education in general (about which more, shortly), I fear that merely adding this or that theory, fact, or principle from cognitive science to the curriculum of teachers will only add to the mess teacher training is in. I thus advocate the *study* of cognition for teachers.

The plan for what follows is: in the next chapter, I diagnose 'education' as a discipline of some kind, and outline views of knowledge that save education from all the multicultural and relativist water in the sea. This is concluded with the notion that 'applying knowledge' is most fruitfully regarded as another name for 'doing empirical research'. After this, we turn in Chapters 3, 4 and 5 to an outline of what cognition entails, questions about learning, the differences between us, and ways in which the *study* of cognition will improve on what schooling produces.

---

[75] I ignore the pressing question of the financial reward commensurate with such training, as well as other issues that impinge on the quality of the teachers selected for the provision of excellent education.

CHAPTER 2

Applying Knowledge

In the previous chapter I outlined questions and issues to do with the provision of excellent mass education. I also suggested that the proper focus for this is on universally standardised skills, technology, and knowledge. In this chapter I want to find a surer grasp of knowledge and applied knowledge.

It is my contention that knowing about knowledge offers some relief from the pressure exerted by fashionable talk of relativism, pluralism, multiculturalism and so forth. By way of convincing teachers (and teachers of teachers) that a sure grasp of *knowledge* is a first step towards placing education where it belongs, I consider education as a *discipline*. After this, I turn to a discussion of knowledge and applied knowledge.

2.1 Positioning education

In my view, 'education', as a place-holder for that which a teacher must *know* and do in addition to possessing subject-specific expertise, is really a melange of common sense, homeopathic recipes, titbits from here, there and everywhere, and knowledge amassed from more traditional disciplines like philosophy, psychology, and sociology.

The uncritical use of common sense or the application of mere guesses, fashionable ideas, and know-how about people, as well as the use of tried and tested 'rules of thumb' without the ongoing empirical assessment of the success of these, pose a definite threat to the epistemic integrity of education (as a discipline). I want to call this 'canned' common sense[1] because I believe that these guesses become fossilised, in time and place, as the taken-for-granted way things are.[2] I would further speculate that the unquestionable use of common sense in the classroom comes from the fact that people, in order to get by, and as a way of getting along with others in a social world, have to be *au fait* with people and social situations,[3] in both general and particular situations. On the face of it, therefore, teachers do not need *extra* knowledge on how to handle their charges in the classroom.

It also takes only a moment's reflection to acknowledge that not all people

---

[1] Geertz, C., *Local Knowledge. Further Essays in Interpretative Anthropology* (New York: Basic Books, 1983), 84, claims that common sense as a cultural system and as sources of knowledge might just be as totalising as any other system of ideas. As he puts it, 'no religion is more dogmatic, no science more ambitious, no philosophy more general'; he also lists the following characteristics of common sense: naturalness, an 'air of, of-courseness' (85), i.e. that things are simply as they are; practicalness in the sense of sagacity, to be 'prudent, level-headed (and to) keep (your) eye on the ball' (87); thinness, i.e. 'the world is what the wide-awake, uncomplicated person takes it to be' (89); immethodicalness, which caters for both 'the pleasures of inconsistency' and 'the intractable diversity of experience' (90); and accessibleness, i.e. 'the insistence that any person with faculties reasonably intact can grasp common-sense conclusions ... (and) will not only grasp them but embrace them' (91). Contrast this with the following: 'Firstly, the world just is not constructed on a common-sensical basis. This means that "natural" thinking – ordinary, day-to-day common sense – will never give an understanding about the nature of science. Scientific ideas are, with rare exceptions, counter-intuitive: they cannot be acquired by simple inspection of phenomena and are often outside everyday experience. Secondly, doing science requires a conscious awareness of the pitfalls of "natural" thinking for common sense is prone to error when applied to problems requiring rigorous and quantitative thinking; lay theories are highly unreliable'; Wolpert, L., *The Unnatural Nature of Science* (Cambridge, MA: Harvard University Press, 1997), xi–xii.

[2] In advocating the experimental-developmental method, which involves, *inter alia*, the analysis of process rather than objects, Vygotsky has this to say about the problem of 'fossilized behavior': '... in psychology we often meet with processes that have already died away, that is, processes that have gone through a very long stage of historical development and have become fossilized'; it is then the task of the analyst, through the appropriate method, to reconstruct or at best provoke this process; Vygotsky, L.S., *Mind in Society. The Development of Higher Psychological Processes*, Cole, M., John-Steiner, V., Scribner, S. and Souberman, E. (eds.) (Cambridge, MA: Harvard University Press, 1978), 58–64.

[3] The notion that we have a module – hardwired over evolutionary time – for dealing with people, called a 'Theory of Mind', is a topic of ongoing interest. Cf. Carpendale, J.I.M. and Lewis, C., 'Constructing an understanding of mind: The development of children's social understanding within social interaction', *Behavioral and Brain Sciences*, 27 (2004), 79–151.

are equally good at getting by, that some are hopeless, others supremely good at it, and most of us fall somewhere in between – perhaps depending on the people (e.g. normal or damaged, children, adults, or the aged), and the situations before us (e.g. intimate interactions, social exchanges with strangers, or with very different 'others'). This, again, suggests that perhaps there is indeed some knowledge – over and above common sense – that those dealing with people need in order to get by. The question is: what kind of knowledge do teachers need in order to cope with the business of the classroom: learning and teaching?

The question is thus: what do our natural abilities as people, boosted by interest (some choosing to work with people or to become teachers), sometimes *lack* that must be supplied through disciplines such as cognitive science to turn a mathematician, for example, into a teacher of mathematics?

One could argue that it is hoped that professional training supplements the repertoire of the newcomer with formal theories, facts or principles in the absence of relevant experience; or that it adds what experience would have, and will in time. Does this suffice, however, to justify the 'what' and 'how' of professional training? One could also argue that the 'extra' stuff a teacher gets through her teacher training serves as a preparation for teachers regarding what to expect, so as to prevent undue surprises when encountering strange or new situations, or specific kinds of pathologies (e.g. dyslexia, childhood depression, symptoms of abuse), in the classroom or among the pupils. This is reasonable as far as this kind of preparation goes, but it never goes much further than our ordinary, human intuitions regarding normality/abnormality. I had this in mind when referring above to 'homeopathic recipes', i.e. the extremely watered-down dosage of knowledge that in the end gets added to the repertoire of teachers. It is this kind of watered-down knowledge, probably a consequence of the duration and nature of 'teacher training', that is a problem for what I want to propose in later chapters too. For this reason I insist on the *study* of cognition, or familiarity with questions, debates and issues involved in cognition,[4] rather than a focus on this or that 'theory' or set of principles about learning and other relevant concerns for schooling; more about this in Chapters 3, 4 and 5.

Our common sense also tends to endorse some ideas and stories about people more readily than others. This is a problem in the absence of knowledge about knowledge, as well as in the absence of a thorough grounding in what makes learning possible and effective. Consider best-sellers on topics such as emotional intelligence, practical intelligence,[5] and various other forms of intelligence[6] as well as the sometimes highly suspect programmes and motivational courses aimed at improving one's 'people skills'. Do those who support any of these actually know about knowledge, or have an empirical or evidential basis for their support?

The notion of multiple intelligences[7] was made famous in the early '80s by the famous (and very popular) writer on education, Howard Gardner.[8] Whether any of these 'talents' really ought to count as a distinct ability to solve problems efficiently and effectively and, as such, really ought to be regarded as independent of the general factor[9] identified in studies of intelligence, is not as clear as

---

[4] This is also the basis of my defence against Spurrett's charge in the Preface that Chapter 3 has rather *too much* philosophy. In other words, given the problems I identify, it is imperative to propose a remedy that is to some extent immune from these.
[5] Cf. http://www.psy.pdx.edu/PsiCafe/KeyTheorists/Sternberg.htm#Papers .
[6] Cf. http://www.eiconsortium.org/ .
[7] Cf. Gardner, H., *Intelligence Reframed: Multiple Intelligences for the 21st Century* (New York: Basic Books, 1999); Gardner, H., *Multiple Intelligences: The Theory into Practice* (New York: Basic Books, 1993); Gardner, H., *Frames of Mind: The Theory of Multiple Intelligences* (New York: Basic Books, 1983); and Willingham, D.T., 'Reframing the mind: Howard Gardner became a hero among educators simply by redefining talents as "intelligences"', *Education Next* (Summer 2004).
http://www.findarticles.com/p/articles/mi_m0MJG/is_3_4/ai_n6143580#continue .
[8] For Gardner's many publications, see: http://www.pz.harvard.edu/PIs/HGpubs.htm .
[9] This is defined, nowadays, by experts, as follows: 'General intelligence is ... the covariation cutting across various problem solving mediums (numerical, pictorial, verbal), assessment modalities (group, individual), and populations (cross culturally); it reflects the general factor – or commonality – shared by these multiple operations'; Lubinski, D., 'Scientific and social significance of assessing individual differences: "Sinking shafts at a few critical points"', *Annual Review of Psychology*, 51 (2000), 412; see also Jensen, A.R., *The G Factor. The Science of Mental Ability* (London: Praeger, 1998).

Gardner's popularity (itself sanctioned by the common sense of people about themselves and others) would suggest. My point is that our common sense about ourselves goes a long way in education from lay to expert pronouncements, on issues such as intelligence and more, and serves to highlight particular projects and not others. This has its uses, to be sure, but it also has distinct limitations in the classroom.

Those who are called on to become teachers or who drift towards this endeavour rarely if ever obtain, through their 'educational studies' or 'teacher training', a thorough grounding in the epistemic and cognitive business of their task. This is probably partly due to the teacher's qualification being thought of as more of a union membership or certification process than a necessary part of the education of the teacher (who has, after all, already 'graduated' with specific subject expertise).

There is thus some danger that if any knowledge (in some watered-down form or other) is merely added to the melange of bits and pieces from here, there and everywhere that usually make up teacher training, this will simply serve to worsen things – that is to say, it will merely *boost* education's tendency to violate all kinds of methodological, conceptual, and epistemological boundaries, as well as logical rules, in the 'application' of rootless ideas to classroom practices. In other words, merely adding knowledge will simply serve to promote the tendency to misuse ideas by applying them out of their proper knowledge-base; or the tendency to read theories as pictures, metaphors or suggestions about how to tackle this or that education task. And these tendencies lead too easily to the introduction of Piaget/Vygotsky/the latest and greatest hero 'into the classroom' – i.e. into the one place theorists/theories generally do not belong without some further research. It is in view of these problems that I concern myself with the *application* of knowledge in the last section of this chapter.

As a department at training colleges or universities, 'education' often houses a mini-university; that is to say, the staff/faculty of schools/departments of education have some basic familiarity with parts of the traditional disciplines, and profess on these to their students. As members of this mini-university they, then, tend to create hybrids like 'math-education'. The latter is presented as something distinct from mathematics as a discipline, and from cognition[10] as the name for studies of learning, thinking and knowing. In this way, education gains a certain status from its association with and appropriation of more traditional disciplines. It further adds to this the more practical arts associated with teachers-in-practice. For example, teacher training often includes exposure to *doing* English language teaching, geography, or physical science, thus tapping into the much vaunted experiential basis to education.

It is my contention, however, that these associations and appropriations are nothing more than permissive dips into and out of the arts and sciences. Moreover, these allow education to function in an in-between terrain – a murky terrain that sanctions neither science (which would compel education to have its claims brought before the tribunal of truth[11]), nor philosophy (which would force education to engage in the critical task of conceptual clarification). Further, this positioning places education at the bottom of the pile as far as news from the hardier disciplines goes. That is to say, education is usually the last to consume and adjust to epistemic shifts from elsewhere in the knowledge matrix. An example of this is the ongoing life, among educators, or educational experts, of attachments to fashionable nonsense such as various anti-scientific and postmodern stances.

Unregulated by ideals such as truth and knowledge, or conceptual rigour, education is thus cast adrift without protection against the political visions (or politically correct talk) of a time and place. This is a problem, at least in the sense

---

[10] See Green, C.D., 'Where did the word "cognitive" come from anyway?', *Canadian Psychology*, 37 (1996), 31–9.

[11] As a case in point, consider Howard Gardner writing 'that schools are very complex institutions and the processes of learning that are supposed to take place there over months and years are difficult to capture in scientific research' (and this after underlining his life-long involvement in 'a school of education' and commitment 'to school reform'). http://www.findarticles.com/p/articles/mi_qa3671/is_200401/ai_n9380545/ .

that with the advent of mass education, and the explosion of available and accessible information, we need to *know* the relevant benefit of schooling. Knowing when to or even whether to leave well alone (in classrooms, on the street, or in the homes of learners), versus deliberately intervening in people's lives from birth to death matter enough to know what and how to do this best.

Education is also increasingly under pressure to deliver the goods in terms of producing the skills and knowledge necessary for successful lives, and in terms of addressing the differences between us and our hope for a more egalitarian future. Phrased differently, if a society lacks technological skills, if there are too few female mathematicians, or if Caucasian males are over-represented in high status professions, it is to education that we turn for at least part of the solution. We reason that if we allow the *status quo* to run its course through the home, street, and classroom, these lacks and imbalances will not be corrected and may even be exacerbated. However, unless education can defend its interventions in terms of good, strong supporting evidence for its claims and doings, how is society to decide on one versus another kind of intervention?

In positioning education, it is thus fair to say that it is at worst nothing but common sense, etc., which does not justify investment in it. And on a slightly more elevated level, education might be thought of as an endeavour rooted in religious instruction and involving those who are committed to teaching, training and instructing the young in what is needed by, and good for, society. Neither of these seems adequate to the increasingly difficult task of preparing learners for successful participation in a complex, global set-up. The study of cognition seems an appropriate addition not only because of conflicting realities coming together in open sites (as noted in Chapter 1), but also because it is uncontroversial that education is about learning (and whatever makes this possible, efficient and appropriate) and its transactive counterpart, teaching (and whatever makes this possible, efficient and appropriate). It is my argument then that cognitive science is at the heart of education – not that this is discernible in the courses/modules on offer within most faculties/schools of education or even in the research output of most departments of education (although there are, of course, notable exceptions[12]). Furthermore, if such a shift is to be taken up properly, then education has to be placed on a more secure epistemic footing.

2.2 Knowledge without borders or owners

I do not believe it makes sense to claim ownership for knowledge,[13] thus, I do not agree with the idea that there is 'western' and 'African' *knowledge* (except in a trivial sense of these terms). Moreover, thinking that the scientific thinking that started about five to four centuries before the Common Era in ancient societies like Greece and China[14] 'belongs' to Europeans and, as such, excludes Africans is nonsense. This clearly does not mean that historically it is of no interest to find answers to: 'who did what first, and where?'. My point is that, once invented, discovered, thought and made public, knowledge does not 'belong' to someone like an object or a private possession belongs to its owner.[15]

I cannot genuinely believe that different cultures (or genders) somehow 'have' different standards and rules for justifying and ratifying beliefs – in a

---

[12] Cf. work by: A. Demetriou and colleagues (Department of Educational Sciences, Cyprus); Leslie Smith (Department of Educational Research, Lancaster University, UK); Vosniadou, S., 'Towards a revised cognitive psychology for new advances in learning and instruction', *Learning and Instruction*, 6/2 (1996), 95–109; and Vosniadou, S., Ioannides, C., Dimitakopoulou, A. and Papademetriou, E., 'Designing learning environments to promote conceptual change in science', *Learning and Instruction*, 11/4–5 (2001), 381–419.

[13] Of course, this is not to deny authorship, intellectual property rights, ownership of things involved in knowledge, or the places and stories, contexts and the sages who remember, store, and transmit folk wisdom and even cures; all of which require (legal) protection and recognition, and payment when bought.

[14] Cf. Lloyd, G.E.R., *Adversaries and Authorities* (Cambridge: CUP, 1996); Lloyd, G.E.R., *Demystifying Mentalities* (Cambridge: CUP, 1990); Lloyd, G.E.R., *The Revolutions of Wisdom* (Berkeley: Berkeley University Press, 1987); Lloyd, G.E.R., *Magic, Reason and Experience* (Cambridge: CUP, 1979); and Lloyd, G.E.R., *Polarity and Analogy* (Cambridge: CUP, 1966).

[15] Cf. Lefkowitz, M., *Not out of Africa. How Afrocentricism Became an Excuse to Teach Myth as History* (New York: Basic Books, 1997).

specific situation, and given similar education.[16] Lastly, I think that possibilities for change, adaptation, and communication across time and space pull the last rug out from under the feet of those who want to locate knowledge claims clearly in a specific (cultural) context with no means of reaching across different contexts through (more or less) objective and neutral evidence. I have argued against an unbreakable bond between culture and knowledge at length elsewhere and do not want to repeat this here.[17] Being ill at ease with the 'Eurocentric' versus 'Afrocentric' tags as far as knowing and knowledge go, does not however mean that I believe different experiences and histories do not express different stories, nor that some of these do not demand more and better hearings; when these are presented and heard, however, they then become part of what is on offer to anyone who cares to know and have knowledge.

The projects I have engaged in since the early '80s in South Africa, like TTT described in Chapter 1, have made me fully aware of the sometimes enormous influences of specific experiences on the way individuals operate in situations and on tasks. This means that I also do not claim that we all act the same regardless of different histories. Our histories show themselves as (1) differences in the habitual ways people operate depending on what is taken-for-granted in a particular group/context/culture; (2) the demands of tasks, which include/exclude or advantage/disadvantage some and not others; and (3) conflicting interpretations of what is 'right' (in the sense of appropriate to know and do) in a given context, or in response to a specific task.[18] Moreover, each of these has many personal and social consequences, educational advantage/disadvantage being one of them. Acknowledging this is not, however,

[16] Haack, S. writes in *Evidence and Inquiry. Towards Reconstruction in Epistemology* (Oxford: Blackwell, 1995), 6: 'the fashionable thesis that different cultures or communities have widely divergent standards of evidence is at least an exaggeration, and possibly altogether false'.
[17] Cf. Craig, A.P., 'Culture and knowledge', *South African Journal of Philosophy*, 20/2 (2001), 191–214.
[18] Cf. Craig (2001); Craig, A.P., 'Education and the question about understanding', *South African Journal of Higher Education*, 15/1 (2001), 25–31; and Craig, A.P., 'The conflict between the familiar and the unfamiliar', *South African Journal of Higher Education*, 3/1 (1989), 166–72.

the same as saying that there are essential differences between, say, men and women, or white and black people – differences that must then be included in what we mean by knowledge, truth, and the justification of the claims made by men, black people, and so on. In addition, acknowledging differences due to different histories or experiences is also not tantamount to saying that, therefore, this knowledge/claim *belongs* to men, this one to women, and so forth.

It is because knowledge, as knowledge, is free of the psychological and cultural moorings of its original authors and context that it is available to all. And it is this very characteristic of knowledge (rather than opinion, common sense, tradition, faith, commitment, and value) that makes it the proper focus for education.[19] Saying all this about knowledge is, however, not the end of the story.

Before Thomas Kuhn's,[20] perhaps unintended,[21] shake-up of debates about knowledge in the last years of the '60s, followed by postmodern and neo-Pragmatist attacks on modernity's picture of knowledge and quest for certainty and ideals such as truth and knowledge,[22] deciding on what counted as *knowledge* was perhaps easier than it is nowadays.[23] I think there is currently afoot a return to more sensible ways, but I do not see this clearly enough in education to want to stop hammering away at all the anti-truth/-knowledge/-science talk about.

So, to repeat, before Kuhn and the rest, separating 'science' from non-science, 'knowledge' from opinion, and dividing claims into relatively clear

---

[19] Craig, A.P., 'Education for all', *South African Journal of Higher Education*, 10/2 (1996), 47–55.
[20] Kuhn, T.S., *The Structure of Scientific Revolutions*, 2nd edn., enlarged (Chicago: University of Chicago Press, 1970).
[21] Cf. Weinberg, S., 'The revolution that didn't happen', *New York Review of Books* (8 October 1998), 48–52.
[22] Cf. Rorty, R., *Truth and Progress. Philosophical Papers* (Cambridge: CUP, 1998).
[23] Toulmin, S., *Cosmopolis. The Hidden Agenda of Modernity* (New York: The Free Press, 1990), 14–35, argues that the 17th century revolution in our thinking is countered by what he calls the 'third phase' of the modern project (or postmodern thinking); the first phase being late Renaissance Humanism, and the second phase being the ideas of the 'new philosophers', notably Galileo, Bacon, and Descartes. For Toulmin, insisting on the power of *rationality*, defined in opposition to 'tradition and superstition', and in terms of decontextualised knowledge, i.e. written, formal logical, universal principles, abstract axioms and timeless theories of the order of things (30–34) does not open up but in fact limits rationality. In his words, 'Rather than expanding the scope of rational or reasonable debate, 17th-century scientists narrowed it' (14, 21, 35).

categories not only seemed an appropriate task, but also one that was, in principle, thought possible. Postmodern discourse, in its finest form, made us aware of the difficulties with finding secure grounds for the criteria or standards we take for granted; standards that are, in fact, part and parcel of the very domain they purport to evaluate. That is to say, this kind of talk about reason made us aware that we tend to use criteria and standards forthcoming from science – for example, to judge some knowledge as (scientifically established) truth, and the rest as non-science and thus falsehoods or unworthy claims to the epithet 'knowledge'.[24] This was a seductive intervention to many, but certainly not as convincing as Thomas Nagel's reply to this kind of thinking.

In *The Last Word*,[25] Nagel presents, in opposition to various forms of subjectivism,[26] an impressive, rationalist account of the objective end to inquiry. The basic question he asks is: where do understanding and justification come to an end? In his words,

> Do they come to an end with objective principles whose validity is independent of our point of view or do they come to an end with our point of view – individual or shared – so that ultimately, even the apparently objective and universal principles derived their validity or authority from the perspective and practice of those who follow them?[27]

Nagel concludes his examination by stating that something can be considered, 'without relativistic qualification true or false, right or wrong, good or bad',[28] thus,

---

[24] Bernstein, R.J., *Beyond Objectivism and Relativism* (Oxford: Blackwell, 1983).
[25] Nagel, T., *The Last Word* (Oxford: OUP, 1997). See also Nagel, T., *The View from Nowhere* (Oxford: OUP, 1986).
[26] Subjectivism involves for him all arguments/positions claiming that what appear to be objective principles for ending inquiry are nothing more than an individual or shared consensus regarding what is valid and has authority. A rationalist answer to this claims that inquiry comes 'to an end with objective principles whose validity is independent of our point of view' (*Ibid.*, 3).
[27] Nagel's arguments establish the mind-independent authority of reason. In his book he states at the outset: 'In order to have the authority it claims, reason must be a form or category of thought from which there is not appeal beyond itself – whose validity is unconditional because it is necessarily employed in every purported challenge to itself. This does not mean that there is no appeal against the results of any particular exercise of reason, since it is easy to make mistakes in reasoning or to be completely at sea about what conclusions it permits us to draw. But the corrections or doubts must come from further applications of reason itself' (*Ibid.*, 3; 8–9).
[28] *Ibid.*, 6.

38

that inquiry comes to an end in objective principles. Central to his argument for universally valid or objective principles is the insight that one cannot just *exit* from the dictates of logic, or get *outside* debates about morality, the results of some or other empirical science, or an arithmetical/mathematical conclusion – any disagreement with the results of these forces one back into first-order ethical, scientific or mathematical reasoning. I would be tempted to leave it at this, but in fairness, I discuss different acknowledgements of the problems related to the contexts of claims, the relevance of the first person (singular or plural) perspective, and the possibility of knowledge, below. I pay scant attention to those after Kuhn (e.g. radical constructivists,[29] sociologists of knowledge, and other 'bullies'[30]) who merely troubled the waters to such a degree that it was thought that 'anything goes'[31] (which means, of course, that power will rule over truth).

The difficulties with getting a secure grip on knowledge, or pinning it down philosophically, have led Williams to question the task of finding a coherent theory of 'knowledge' *in toto*.[32] Phrased differently, seeking a philosophical understanding of knowledge, what it is and how we come to have it, leads us down a sceptical path. As Hume famously remarked, scepticism is 'a malady which can never be radically cur'd' because the more we reflect on our understanding of knowledge or the sources of our knowledge, the more we expose all of these to further doubt.[33] Williams believes this malady to be the product of a 'contentious epistemological theory',[34] one that imposes a totality condition on knowledge (aims to assess all of it, all at once) and one that assumes the absolute priority of experience over knowledge of the world. He writes that,

---

[29] See Hacking, I., *'The Social Construction of What?* (Cambridge, MA: Harvard University Press, 1999).
[30] Cf. Koertge, N. (ed.), *A House Built on Sand: Exposing Postmodernist Myths about Science* (Oxford: OUP, 2000); Sokal, A. and Bricmont, J., *Fashionable Nonsense. Postmodern Intellectuals' Abuse of Science* (New York: Picador, 1998).
[31] Cf. Feyerabend, P., *Against Method* (Bristol: Western Printing Services Ltd, 1975).
[32] Williams, M., *Unnatural Doubts. Epistemological Realism and the Basis of Scepticism* (Princeton, NJ: Princeton University Press, 1996); and Williams, M., 'Understanding human knowledge philosophically', *Philosophy and Phenomenological Research*, LVI/2 (1996), 359–79.
[33] Williams, *Unnatural Doubts*, 359.
[34] *Ibid.*, 251.

... by stepping back from everyday concerns we discover something about our epistemic situation that we are ordinarily unaware of. We discover what Wittgenstein, in a Humean aside, calls 'the groundlessness of our believing'. Scepticism represents the final verdict on our epistemic situation.[35]

Williams seals the issue he wants to address by saying, 'If Hume is right' – that is to say, if scepticism is theoretically unassailable – then

... we shall never achieve a satisfactory philosophical understanding of how human knowledge is possible, since the very quest for such an understanding leads inevitably to the conclusion that knowledge is not possible at all.[36]

His solution turns on his critical analysis of (a) the notion that there are two real, epistemic kinds (i.e. 'beliefs about the external world' and 'experiential beliefs' – the latter being regarded as having priority over the former – with this metaphysical picture, then, becoming the gateway to both scepticism and foundationalist[37] projects); and (b) the imposition of a 'totality condition' by attempting to assess all our knowledge of the world and experiences' adequacy to the task – as if we have a single, permanent, 'epistemic situation'. For Williams, scepticism is therefore the result of a faulty metaphysical picture, that of 'epistemological realism' (a theoretical view of the objects of epistemological investigation). He suggests that, once rid of it, we could get on with knowing and asking about that which we know in a more context-specific way – a way that acknowledges that whenever we ask any one question, we allow others to remain in the background, unasked. This interaction between background beliefs, or

---

[35] *Ibid.*, 360.
[36] *Idem.*
[37] See Bradie, M. and Harms, W., 'Evolutionary Epistemology', in Zalta, E.N. (ed.), *The Stanford Encyclopedia of Philosophy* (Spring 2004 Edition), URL = <http://plato.stanford.edu/archives/spr2004/entries/epistemology-evolutionary/>, who write: 'Traditional epistemology has its roots in Plato and the ancient skeptics. One strand emerges from Plato's interest in the problem of distinguishing between knowledge and true belief. His solution was to suggest that knowledge differs from true belief in being justified. Ancient skeptics complained that all attempts to provide any such justification were hopelessly flawed. Another strand emerges from the attempt to provide a reconstruction of human knowledge showing how the pieces of human knowledge fit together in a structure of mutual support. This project got its modern stamp from Descartes and comes in empiricist as well as rationalist versions which in turn can be given either a foundational or coherentist twist.'

40

unasked questions, and beliefs for which we can obtain good strong supporting evidence, is given a particularly attractive form in the work of Susan Haack, to which we turn below.[38]

Rorty[39] attempts to push Williams further along the contextualist line (or the position that all beliefs can only be validated *in situ*), and closer to Davidson's attack on the 'scheme-content' distinction[40] through his thesis 'that most of our beliefs – most of anybody's beliefs – must be true'.[41] Rorty clarifies this somewhat controversial statement in the following:

> [Davidson's theoretical] diagnosis [of scepticism] says that the reason the sceptic thinks she needs an inference from experience to the world is that she does not understand that ascription of experience to herself requires ascribing intentional states and that that is possible only for someone who has many true beliefs about the world. There is no such thing as knowing what you believe without knowing a great deal about the objects of your belief.[42]

Again, we see the instability of knowledge in the face of the unasked questions, our background beliefs, or those beliefs that 'stand fast' when we embark on knowing. Rorty thinks Williams is still too attached to the old idea that there is something interesting to say about 'human knowledge' – even when he has (partially, Rorty argues) stripped epistemology of its 'all at once, and once-and-for-all' demands for certainty.

Rorty thus wants us to take the pragmatists' line and talk about more or less useful vocabularies and better and worse solutions to problems. In this regard, he offers Davidson's anti-scheme-content view as a way of ridding us of the habit whereby truth is thought to be 'over there, where the object is, and justification over here, where we are'; he thinks the substitute picture tells us that:

… wherever you have either justification or true beliefs or rationality, you

---

[38] Haack, *Evidence and Inquiry*.
[39] Rorty, *Truth and Progress*.
[40] *Ibid.*, 157.
[41] *Ibid.*, 25.
[42] *Ibid.*, 159.

automatically have a lot of the other two. There is a human activity called 'justifying beliefs' that can be studied historically and sociologically, but this activity does not have a goal called truth or, therefore, a goal called Knowledge. So the question of whether and how we reach this goal does not arise.[43]

Rorty thus calls on us to give up on regulative ideals such as truth and knowledge. But, if we grant this view, we undermine *all* theories of knowledge, *including* those that compete with so-called 'western, white, male, heterosexual' ones. In addition, we give up on questions about knowledge and attempts to improve on the evidential bases for our beliefs. This is clearly where Rorty wants to take us and is also the point of Haack subtitling her book 'towards reconstructing epistemology'.[44] Rorty wants to do something more worthwhile than play epistemic games, while defenders of these games want to find apt ways to characterise our projects aimed at justifying and ratifying beliefs.

I am particularly convinced by Haack's view of knowledge. She outlines the rival theories of epistemic justification, viz. foundationalism and coherentism, by way of proposing another way, standing somewhere between these two. She wants a theory, in her own words:

… which allows the relevance of experience to empirical justification without requiring any beliefs to be justified by experience alone, and which allows pervasive mutual support among beliefs without requiring that empirical justification be a matter exclusively of relations among beliefs.[45]

Haack thus seeks a theory that will 'avoid the difficulties of both foundationalism and coherentism'.[46] Towards this aim she rejects mathematical proof as the ruling metaphor as far as the structure of evidence goes, and proposes instead the crossword puzzle. This, she shows, gives a handle on mutual support that is not viciously circular; she finds 'that the distinction between clues and completed entries parallel(ed) that between experiential evidence and reasons'. She also

[43] *Ibid.*, 163.
[44] Haack, *Evidence and Inquiry*.
[45] Haack, S., *Manifesto of a Passionate Moderate* (Chicago: University of Chicago Press, 1998), 143.
[46] *Idem.*

42

points out that the analogy of the crossword puzzle made her realise 'how deep-seated disagreements in background beliefs will give rise to disagreements about what evidence counts as relevant'.[47] Moreover, she writes that,

> Awareness that others take different background beliefs for granted, and so make different judgements of the worth of this or that evidence, can prompt the realization that your own judgements of the worth of evidence depend on your background beliefs, and are only as good as those beliefs are secure.[48]

In thus acknowledging the role of background beliefs, Haack outlines constraints on knowing, but not the impossibility of truth or knowledge. Moreover, it is on the presumed intractability of differences in background beliefs that epistemological multiculturalism, relativism, and a general despondency about truth and knowledge rest – differences that are not non-negotiable or outside of the reach of more or less objective evidence, as Haack shows. Incompatible background beliefs will give rise to disagreements about what evidence counts as relevant, because, say, 'they' give credit to astrology and 'we' do not; but this does not entail that 'they' and the rest of us cannot all agree on the objective evidence before us. All of us therefore operate against a set of background beliefs, but this does not mean that we cannot separate relevance from truth. This seems to me to make ample allowance for the context-relevant aspects of knowledge, without going overboard.

Because we are human (i.e. creatures in time and place, with a particular perspective on things, and not omniscient, omnipresent, or omnipotent), we can never be absolutely *certain about our certainty*. Wisdom, as far as knowledge goes, therefore involves us in the ongoing scrutiny of the evidence for beliefs (and of that which makes for good strong supporting evidence), as well as the relationship between good evidence and the truth of our beliefs. It is in these terms that I find Haack's 'foundherentism' an encouraging view of knowledge – not because she promises what knowledge cannot deliver, but because she

---

[47] *Idem.*
[48] *Ibid.*, 144.

attempts to show how justification and ratification provide the checks needed in hoping to find truth at the end of ongoing and honest inquiry.[49]

I am not keen on giving up on epistemology, and the quest for certainty from inquiry to inquiry or case to case, and goals such as truth and knowledge, just because the best of current knowledge is unstable in the face of ongoing, scientific investigation. I say this for the reason that there is much that is known that makes a difference to our lives; there is much that is non-trivially true, and a great deal of stuff deserving of the epithet 'knowledge'. This does not mean that I am blind to changes in these terms and what striving for them (good and bad) has delivered. It does mean that I believe a goal such as 'knowing the truth' shows itself wherever a wound is sterilised, a telephone answered, a child not beaten because he uses his left hand to write, or a woman given a job she deserves.

These ordinary examples of the products of pursuing the truth about (in these cases) carriers of infections (germs); how things work; the range of normal development; and what all people are capable of (oppressed groups too), are heartening. I therefore want to defend the goal called truth, and the one called knowledge, because I believe these goals get results that more often than not liberate people from the consequences of ignorance. That the scientific worldview (a view committed to the demonstration of beliefs through evidence and argument), which started developing in ancient societies like Greece and China, has not delivered us from all preventable human suffering is perhaps disappointing, but hardly grounds for rejecting scientific thinking as a universal path to truth.

I hope that the above review of some problems about knowledge (e.g. the import of faulty epistemic pictures, and the role of un-asked questions or our background beliefs), and issues worth thinking about (e.g. how far to go along the contextualist line without going overboard and losing goals such as truth

---

[49] Haack has this apt quotation from William James at the start of the last chapter of her *Evidence and Inquiry*: '[W]hen ... we give up the doctrine of objective certitude, we do not thereby give up the quest or hope of truth itself' (203).

altogether) allows me to conclude that there are apt frameworks for holding onto an ideal like knowledge. So that, even though we have come to appreciate that we cannot secure truth and knowledge – for all time and place – against change and the differences between us, we know that we can rely on our human ability to find, evaluate and discuss the evidence before 'us' *and* 'them'. We are thus up to the task of completing the crossword puzzle in view of evidence that is more or less objective, depending on the manner in which background beliefs are kept in check, and the degree to which the dictates of scientific research are followed, and so on.[50] The important point to emphasise is that there are no good and sound reasons for giving up on ideals such as truth and knowledge.

If we follow Williams, then all we need in order to hold onto knowledge is to let go of the faulty metaphysical picture and the totality condition, and we can then proceed with some certainty that what we know is, in fact, true – in this context, under these conditions. And if we follow Haack, we know we must proceed cautiously because of the unasked questions in the background, but that this does not undermine justification and ratification – rather, it underlines their ongoing relevance.

Philosophically speaking, therefore, we need not throw our hands up in despair over cultural differences in background beliefs and the impossibility of absolute truth, or allow ourselves to be cowed before the sceptic, as Williams shows – even though, as he argues, we need to take a more limited, and context-dependent view of 'knowledge'.

Educationally speaking, this suggests to me that justified, true beliefs – knowledge – stands firm enough to be separable from values, interests, concerns and other beliefs to proceed with the task of finding a knowledge base for the business of the shared classroom. Phrased differently, we have the skills, technologies, and knowledge (*about* knowledge, in this case) to secure some

---

[50] See Kuhn, D., 'Is good thinking scientific thinking?', in Olson, D.R. and Torrance, N., *Modes of Thought. Explorations in Culture and Cognition* (Cambridge: CUP, 1996), 261–81.

beliefs and to separate them from those unable to stand the tests of truth and logic. This alone underwrites my hope that teachers, and teachers of teachers, will come to demand more *knowledge* for schooling than the melange of common sense, homeopathic recipes, and titbits from here, there and everywhere that too often defines what a teacher knows in addition to her subject-specific expertise.

We now turn to the *application* of knowledge, having established some grasp of knowledge as such.

2.3 Another name for doing empirical research

My line of reasoning in this section is as follows: unless teachers become committed to research, 'application' will continue to be understood as a licence for promiscuous borrowing from here, there, and everywhere, as outlined above. This obviously has a particular meaning as far as teaching goes. It would be unreasonable to expect teachers, in their study of cognition, to actually undertake empirical research on every problem they encounter in the classroom. My point is, rather, that viewing cognition or cognitive science as the most suitable knowledge base for whatever is supposed to happen through teaching from the standpoint of a *researcher*, involves the teacher in the following: (a) reading and thinking about problems hypothetically, i.e. as if answers are not ready-made but possible in view of the best knowledge on a problem; (b) searching for answers with the most empirical and logical support; (c) comparing the selected answers against each other and against their respective outcomes in particular situations; and (d) continuing to search for possible answers through *hypothetical thinking* about the problems in the classroom.[51]

This kind of reorientation to thinking about how to teach demands some faith in the possibility of knowledge, as such, and willingness to: *distance*

---

[51] See Kuhn, 'Is good thinking scientific thinking?' for a description of excellent tools for *reading* research properly or engaging in hypothetical thought.

ourselves from taken-for-granted beliefs and practices and to uphold *methods* and *forms* of thought specifically aimed at truth and knowledge. Or phrased in summary fashion, this kind of approach requires a willingness to follow the dictates of *logic*.[52] The ideal is thus that teachers will act and think like researchers about the problems before them. This does not mean that they have to discover the proverbial wheel afresh, but it does mean that any attempt at a straightforward application of this or that idea to the classroom is bound to fail.

There is clearly nothing wrong with *applying*[53] knowledge. Moreover, a great deal of good comes from using knowledge to solve practical problems – some will go so far as to say that this is the best or even the only reason to pursue knowledge at all.[54]

---

[52] 'Simple logical thoughts dominate all others and are dominated by none, because there is no intellectual position we can occupy from which it is possible to scrutinize those thoughts without presupposing them. That is why they are exempt from scepticism: they cannot be put into question by an imaginative process that essentially relies on them.' ... 'the consequences of this kind of dominance include more than the impossibility of scepticism. They include the impossibility of any sort of relativistic, anthropological, or "pragmatist" interpretation. To say that we cannot get outside them means that the last word, with respect to such beliefs, belongs to the content of the thought itself rather than to anything that can be said about it'; Nagel, *The Last Word*, 64.

[53] Quick definitions: Applied science:
- noun: the discipline dealing with the art or science of applying scientific knowledge to practical problems. Applied science is the exact science of applying knowledge from one or more natural scientific fields to practical problems. It is closely related or identical to engineering. Applied science can be used to develop technology.

Quick definitions: Applied mathematics:
- noun: the branches of mathematics that are involved in the study of the physical or biological or sociological world. Applied mathematics is a branch of mathematics that concerns itself with the application of mathematical knowledge to other domains. Such applications include numerical analysis, mathematics of engineering, linear programming, optimisation and operations research, continuous modelling, mathematical biology and bioinformatics, information theory, game theory, probability and statistics, financial mathematics, actuarial science, cryptography and hence combinatorics and even finite geometry to some extent, graph theory as applied to network analysis, and a great deal of what is called computer science. The question of what is applied mathematics does not answer to logical classification so much as to the sociology of professionals who use mathematics. The mathematical methods are usually applied to the specific problem field by means of a mathematical model of the system.

http://en.wikipedia.org/w/index.php?title=Special:Allpages&from=Apple_propagation .

[54] Toulmin, *Cosmopolis*, 184, captures this in a debate about 'excellence' versus 'relevance' as follows: 'The spokesmen for *relevance* [were of the opinion that] it was not valuable to keep our knowledge oiled, clean, and sharpened ... it was more important to find ways of putting it to work for human good. From this standpoint, the universities should attack the practical problems of

I do not support the call for relevance to the exclusion of pursuing knowledge for knowledge's sake,[55] but I do have a quarrel with applying ideas without the status of knowledge (justified true beliefs) or with very flimsy empirical support. Further, the kind of problems confronted in the classroom, the nature of theory, as such, and the status of available theories for classroom problems compel us to take another line. By way of clarification, consider what theories do, in general.

> Theories reach beyond their grasp to predict the existence of previously unsuspected phenomena. They generate hypotheses, disciplined guesses about unexplored topics whose parameters the theories help to define. The best theories generate the most fruitful hypotheses, which translate cleanly into questions that can be answered by observation and experiment.[56]

What is crucial in this view of theoretical work is that the entities posited are testable against 'the acid washes of scepticism, experiment, and the claims of rival theories'.[57] When education thus deals in entities that are both conceptually/philosophically and empirically unexamined, or puts to use ideas that have not undergone the acid washes outlined, these practices are, to say the least, of a dubious status.

Generally speaking, therefore, theorising involves a movement of thought from particulars to abstractions (by way of formulating laws, principles), while the demands of application, again, effectively involve a re-tracing of this movement back to the particular. So, unless such re-tracing to the particular is

---

humanity: if the established disciplines served as obstacles in this enterprise, new interdisciplinary styles of work were needed, that would be better adapted to this task. The inherited corpus of knowledge was no doubt excellent in its way, but academics in the 1970s could no longer afford to behave like Mandarins. "Learning [it was said] is too important to be left to the Learned".' Cf. Craig, A.P., 'To live for a future', *Psychology in Society*, 25 (1999), 37–56 and 63–4; cf. also Hoggart, R., *The Way We Live Now* (London: Chatto and Windus, 1995) for a more jaundiced view and one closer to my own. Hoggart writes on relativism that it 'leads to populism which then leads to levelling; and so to reductionism, to quality-reductionism of all kinds – from food to moral judgments' (8).
[55] Cf. Craig, A.P., 'Really virtual/Virtually real', in Bensusan, D. (ed.), *W(h)ither the University* (Kenwyn: Juta and Co. Ltd, 1996), 62–73.
[56] Wilson, E.O., *Consilience. The Unity of Knowledge* (London: Abacus, 1998), 57.
[57] *Ibid.*, 56.

48

accompanied by ongoing scientific scrutiny,[58] we lose too much in the back and forth between abstraction and application. Think about applying the following principle or statement: *People who were abused as children often grow up abusing their own children.* If this has to be applied, as is, to an individual case, it will more often than not violate not only the explicit scope of the generalisation, but also the reality of the particular, individual case. If these two sets of moves (in whichever direction) from the particular to the general, or the concrete to the abstract, are unchecked by *empirical* tests and inferential *logic*, the resultant 'knowledge' is truly a hotchpotch of who knows what. This is a dangerous terrain if the teacher is led to feel secure in using ideas from a mother discipline (e.g. psychology[59]), which claims a certain scientific status for itself.[60]

In addition, the data-theory gap in social science means that the user of a theory always has to confront the issue of competing theories concerning the same phenomenon.[61] Phrased differently, applications from the social sciences are always exposed to alternative explanations, each perhaps with the same or equal empirical weight. Working with existing theories thus involves ongoing empirical examination of the facts, principles, or sets of ideas that are to be applied. Further, dealing with ill-structured or open-ended problems[62] – the kind of problems

---

[58] Cf. Kuhn, 'Is good thinking scientific thinking?'.
[59] Quick definitions: Applied psychology:
   • noun: any of several branches of psychology that seek to apply psychological principles to practical problems of education or industry or marketing etc. The basic premise of 'applied psychology' is the use of psychological principles and theories to overcome practical problems in other fields, such as business management, product design, ergonomics, nutrition or clinical medicine.
http://en.wikipedia.org/w/index.php?title=Special:Allpages&from=Apple_propagation .
[60] Cf. http://www.apa.org/about/ and http://www.bps.org.uk/ .
[61] In using facts, principles and theories from the 'hard' sciences, or from fields of study where the empirical basis for the knowledge accumulated is indeed very strong, some of the problems discussed here are less worrisome as far as application goes. This, then, might be another reason for tying education more directly to cognitive *science*, especially to the hard data forthcoming from the brain sciences, for example.
[62] Cf. Strohm-Kitchener, K. 'Cognition, metacognition, and epistemic cognition. A three-level model of cognitive processing', *Human Development*, 26, (1983), 222–32.

typical of education – means that choosing this or that theory is not all that simple or only dependent on someone's creative insight.[63]

The most obvious solution to the problems outlined is to turn facts, principles, and theories from a suitable domain of knowledge into hypotheses for further study. I say this in view of the kind of knowledge most typically available for application to education, the nature of theorising, the demands of the particular, and the gap between theory and its evidential support. Moreover, the disciplined use of existing knowledge to formulate testable hypotheses for classroom problems will at best lead to a steady accumulation of organised, systematic knowledge on the problems before us. The most important constraint on application, therefore, is the need to do, or at least be informed by, *empirical research*. This is not a calamity but rather a sure way for education to elevate its scientific status. Application conceived in this way could generate theoretical work of the highest order. Vygotsky's own research, to which we turn briefly below and more fully in subsequent chapters, represents, as far as I am concerned, theoretical work of this order.

When a straight-through application *does* occur (i.e. without empirical examination and monitoring of the entity posited, its empirical support, and its usefulness to a classroom issue), it is usually of the kind where someone decides to use, say, 'constructivism' as a method of teaching because the notion is seemingly sanctioned by 'Piaget's constructivism'. But this is to get application wrong, to get Piaget's use of constructivism wrong,[64] and indeed (and perhaps more dangerously) to get learning wrong.[65]

---

[63] Wolpert, *The Unnatural Nature of Science*, 56–84, contrasts creativity in the arts, with that in science, and underlines the hard work (e.g. data-gathering, description, explanation and theory-testing) that comes *after* the truly novel guess, insight, or bright idea that might start a process of discovery in science: 'Creativity in the arts is characteristically intensely personal and reflects both the feelings and the ideas of the artist. By contrast, scientific creativity is always constrained by self-consistency, by trying to understand nature and by what is already known'.

[64] Cf. Kitchener, R.F., *Piaget's Theory of Knowledge. Genetic Epistemology and Scientific Reason* (New Haven: Yale University Press, 1986).

[65] Cf. Gardner, H., 'The New New Math', *New York Review of Books*, 45/14 (24 September 1998).

50

If someone wants to check whether children can indeed 'construct' some or other basic idea in, say, mathematics or science from within their own resources or on their own, i.e. without input/instruction from someone or something else, this demands controlled comparisons, the generation of data/evidence, and the logical tests of inferences from data to conclusion, in the usual manner of testing a hypothesis.[66] To give another example, if a 'constructivist pedagogy' (whatever someone could take this to mean!) is to be *applied* in the manner outlined above, this will involve empirical research aimed at the dual task of (a) assessing the (suitably operationalised) idea, as such (a 'constructivist pedagogy'), and (b) putting this, now as a hypothesis about, say, novel learning on some or other task, to further scrutiny – if indeed (a) delivered the goods to proceed with (b). My point is thus that the *application* of knowledge is at best another name for *doing empirical research*.

By way of illustrating the *application* of knowledge further, allow me to reiterate the primary questions behind my own empirical research into learning, i.e. (1) what does the task demand in terms of skills and knowledge, and (2) what do learners need to *know* and *do* in order to succeed with the task at hand? This, to anyone who knows Vygotsky's work,[67] is an application of his theory of learning, which involves the central idea of a 'zone of proximal development' (ZPD). Vygotsky clarifies the ZPD in the following terms: it is

> ... the distance between the actual developmental level as determined by independent problem-solving and the level of potential development as determined through problem-solving under adult guidance or in collaboration with more capable peers.[68]

The application of this allowed for the generation of novel data, which required further analysis, in order to design a learning-teaching situation with the appropriate form and content for the problem under examination (and the latter,

---

[66] See Kuhn, 'Is good thinking scientific thinking?' for a fine elaboration of the method and logic involved, as well as typical errors committed by novices, in such testing.
[67] Vygotsky, *Mind in Society*.
[68] *Ibid.*, 86.

too, required ongoing monitoring and analysis of data generated). I mention this to underline the relationship between knowledge and application in education. Phrased differently, it is scientifically unwise to attempt a straight-through application of most facts, principles, and theories available to education – even when the theorist, Vygotsky in this case, has considerable authority as a theorist.

And on another tack, it is the case that what we take schooling to involve (what is taught, how this is done, and so on) too easily becomes *set* in the shape of a specific, age-/stage-appropriate curriculum, and method of teaching.[69] This set shape or the content-specific focus (e.g. mathematics), teaching method(s) (e.g. small-group teaching or 'sage on stage'), and so on, only come up for review *when something goes wrong* (e.g. when Johnny does not learn to read, count, or whatever), when something changes (e.g. the advent of multicultural classrooms with conflicting demands on teachers or schooling), or when a new fashion presses for address (e.g. the New New Math).

It seems that a more clearly *research* orientated focus, or thinking of application as *doing empirical research*, will also assist in this situation. It is so that knowledge (and technology as well as the skills demanded for using these) has attained a run-away quality over the last decades. In addition, new events or discoveries have an influence on what is on offer to anyone who can access, understand and use these. For example, prevalence of news about our genetic heritage, and the prominence of genetic studies generally, are examples of a certain shift in many people's self-understanding (perhaps due to attention given in the media to the completion of the Human Genome Project[70] and the cloning of Dolly the sheep[71]). My concern is that as disciplines (and thus bodies of expertise) advance and take on a new content and form, what is understood by learning,

---

[69] From Frankena's characterisation of education as involving: (1) *teaching* (2) *learning* (3) the *result* produced in the one being educated, and (4) the discipline or study [once called 'pedagogics'] – the 'what' and 'how' above could be seen as (3) and (1), where (1) also implies (2); see http://etext.lib.virginia.edu/cgi-local/DHI/dhi.cgi?id=dv2-08 .
[70] Cf. http://www.ornl.gov/sci/techresources/Human_Genome/home.shtml .
[71] Cf. http://www.ornl.gov/sci/techresources/Human_Genome/elsi/cloning.shtml#whatis .

teaching, classrooms, and schooling has largely remained trapped in the common sense described above.

If education is to keep up to date or in line with important changes in knowledge, a more clearly research focus is certainly called for. It is thus in view of a certain lack in teacher training that I advocate a shift in focus from thinking of the application of knowledge as the *transport*, as it were, of ideas from one or another discipline or theorists' work into the classroom, to thinking of this in terms of *doing empirical research*. If this were to happen, I am sure that the epistemic status of education, as a discipline, would improve too; and in this way, so too would what schooling delivers. As far as the teacher goes, this indicates adopting a *hypothetical approach* to problems in the classroom, as clarified above.

In the next part of this work I introduce cognitive science as a suitable knowledge base for education. I propose that the *study* of learning, thinking, perception, memory, and problem-solving will turn education into a respectable discipline in its own right. That is to say, if the facts, principles and theories from cognitive science are used as hypotheses about various classroom issues/problems, education will establish a firm, empirical basis for its own theorising, will contribute to knowledge about cognition, and will be in a position to justify – scientifically – what, how and why Johnnie learns (or not) through schooling.

CHAPTER 3

The Study of Cognition

In this part of the book I want to pursue the idea that a subject-specific expert is turned into a *teacher* through the *study of cognition*.[1] Given the precarious positioning of education as a discipline and the way this affects teacher training, I am however loath to present *this* cognitive theory or *that* fact about cognition or cognitive science[2] as definitive answers. I therefore believe that teachers would do better if, rather than adopting a specific theory or theories about cognition, they had some grasp of the questions and issues involved in learning, thinking, perception, memory, and knowing.

In the previous chapter I examined the idea that teacher training – and as a consequence schooling – will be improved once teachers approach knowledge philosophically, and applied knowledge like scientists. That is to say, I argued that education does *not* have to be crippled by fashionable talk about relativism, etc., and that the improvement of learning is possible through relying on practices that are supported by good, strong empirical evidence.

---

[1] I want to thank Jerry Fodor for his willingness to respond to my email requests for clarification and M.H. Bickhard and A. Demetriou for their responses to my requests for papers.
[2] Cf. Thagard, P., 'Cognitive Science', in Zalta, E.N. (ed.), *The Stanford Encyclopaedia of Philosophy* (Winter 2004 Edition), URL = <http://plato.stanford.edu/archives/win2004/entries/cognitive-science/> .

In this chapter I present different views or overviews of the study of cognition in order to *outline* a domain of study for teachers' purposes. In the next two chapters, I focus the point of the current chapter more clearly: in Chapter 4, on *learning*; and in Chapter 5, on the *differences* between us.

Differences of all kinds are part and parcel of multicultural societies, mass education, and therefore classrooms. In fact, they define the one side of global exchanges across borders; the other being defined by *universal standardisation*. It is then also the tension between differences and universal standardisation that presents a particular set of problems for mass education – problems that are best understood in terms of the study of cognition, as I intend to show and argue in this part of the book. Further, if *learning* begged no questions, if all people learned all tasks equally well, and if education furnished all participants and all societies equally well with the wherewithal to cope with what is on offer globally, this book would have had no point.[3] But given the differences between us, learning in shared classrooms shows up the manner in which the history of specific tasks[4] advantages some and disadvantages others. This offends our egalitarian intuitions, and we will return to it in the next two chapters.

If the focus in schooling is on universally standardised skills, technology and knowledge (as I argue it should be if schooling is to equip learners with the wherewithal to engage what is on offer and to participate successfully in global exchanges),[5] then learning and the differences between us both become central concerns in the study of cognition or, then, applied cognition.

---

[3] It must also be noted that the point I think it has – i.e. that cognitive science has something to offer attempts to improve on what happens during schooling, in particular, learning (and teaching) – depends on how certain one is that there are, in fact, theories, principles, or facts in cognitive science that have serious implications for the various (mental) processes involved in schooling.
[4] I use 'task' to refer to any situation, problem, or encounter that demands (implicitly or explicitly) specific operations, knowledge or information to be engaged at all, and especially to be engaged successfully (e.g. to use a key to unlock a door).
[5] This focus might seem to some an unfair way of giving credit to 'winning' forms and strategies (skills, technology, knowledge). My only response is: yes, indeed. It would seem madness to focus schooling on 'losing' forms and strategies when dealing with both limited resources and multiple

In view of the role I give to the study of cognition, it is important to reiterate that this cognitive section is not offered as a final answer to the many problems that beset education, globally. It is also not offered as the only approach to what cognition is about and to how this discipline could assist the teacher. The overviews presented below are meant as an outline of a discipline, as highlighting important beacons that define the study of cognition.

3.1 Cognition then and now

Cognitive science is alive and well and has been growing steadily over the last few decades (unlike the dead or dying field of 'pedagogics'). The birth date of cognitive science is usually given around the time that Noam Chomsky[6] took on Skinnerian behaviourism,[7] although Jean Piaget's work on cognitive development probably influenced psychologists more.[8] As the well-known story goes, Skinner thought that one learned a language like one learns anything else,[9] through responses to stimuli. Chomsky's review of *Verbal Behavior*[10] not only questioned this view, but in the process loosened the grip of behaviourism[11] on psychology

---

(often competing and conflicting) values, beliefs, identifications, home languages – in short, different cultures – in open, shared sites such as the classrooms of mass education.

[6] Cf. Chomsky, N., *Language and Mind* (New York: Harcourt, Brace and World, 1968); Derwing, B.L., *Transformational Grammar as a Theory of Language Acquisition* (Cambridge: CUP, 1973); and Pinker, S., *The Language Instinct* (New York: Harper Collins, 1994).

[7] Chomsky, N., 'Review of Skinner's *Verbal Behavior*', *Language*, 35 (1959), 26–58.

[8] Piaget, J., *Adaptation and Intelligence: Organic Selection and Phenocopy* (Chicago: University of Chicago Press, 1980); Piaget, J., *The Development of Thought*, trans. A. Rosin. (Oxford: Basil Blackwell, 1977); Piaget, J., *The Psychology of Intelligence* (New Jersey: Littlefield, Adams and Co., 1976); and Vuyk, R., *Overview and Critique of Piaget's Genetic Epistemology 1965–1980. Volumes One and Two* (London: Academic Press, 1981).

[9] In taking Dawkins's 'hill climbing' notion apart, Fodor has the following humorous piece on Skinner's view of verbal learning: 'Babbling is vocal behaviour that's produced at random. When you happen to make a noise that sounds sort of like the local dialect, "society" reinforces you; and your propensity to make that sort of sound (or better, your propensity to make that sort of sound in those sorts of circumstances) increases correspondingly. Keep it up and soon you'll be able to say "Carnegie Hall" or "Jasha Heifitz" or any other of the innumerable things that being able to speak English allows you to say'; Fodor, J.A., *In Critical Condition. Polemical Essays on Cognitive Science and the Philosophy of Mind* (Cambridge, MA: The MIT Press, 1998), 164.

[10] Skinner, B.F., *Verbal Behavior* (New York: Appleton-Century-Crofts, 1957).

[11] See Graham, G., 'Behaviorism', in Zalta, E.N (ed.), *The Stanford Encyclopedia of Philosophy* (Fall 2002 Edition), URL =

and, as such, placed 'the organism' (mind, brain and more recently the body too) back into the study of cognition.[12]

Nowadays, the study of cognition is not only concerned with what is truth-evaluable (i.e. propositions about which one can say that they are either true or false)[13] and no longer takes 'mind' as its only or primary focus. Moreover, theorists have ceased to place cognition in opposition to the other two faculties of 19th century psychology – the will (or volition) and emotion – by increasingly drawing more of the brain, body, words and world into its domain.

This brief introduction to the study of cognition does no more than limn a more or less standard account of how things started, then, and what to expect of things, now. In order to get a somewhat better hold on the discipline, consider Paul Thagard's summary[14] of what the science of cognition is about:

> The central hypothesis of cognitive science is that thinking can best be understood in terms of representational structures in the mind and computational procedures that operate on those structures. While there is much disagreement about the nature of the representations and computations that constitute thinking, the central hypothesis is general enough to encompass the current range of thinking in cognitive science, including connectionist theories which model thinking using artificial neural networks. Most work in cognitive science assumes that the mind has mental representations analogous to computer data structures, and computational procedures similar to computational algorithms. Cognitive theorists have proposed that the mind contains such mental representations as logical propositions, rules, concepts, images, and analogies, and that it uses mental procedures such as deduction, search, matching, rotating, and retrieval. The

---

<http://plato.stanford.edu/archives/fall2002/entries/behaviorism/ >.

[12] 'Mentalistic accounts tend to assume, and sometimes even explicitly to embrace ... the hypothesis that the mind possesses at birth or innately a set of procedures or internally represented processing rules which are deployed when learning or acquiring new responses. Behaviorism, by contrast, is anti-nativist. Behaviorism, therefore, appeals to theorists who deny that there are innate rules by which organisms learn. To Skinner and Watson organisms learn without being innately or pre-experientially provided with explicit procedures by which to learn. Learning does not consist in rule-governed behavior. Learning is what organisms do in response to stimuli. A behaviorist organism learns, as it were, from its successes and mistakes'; Graham, 'Behaviorism'.

[13] Cf. Green, C.D., 'Where did the word "cognitive" come from anyway?', *Canadian Psychology*, 37 (1996), on the meaning and origin of the word 'cognitive'.

[14] Thagard, 'Cognitive Science'.

dominant mind-computer analogy in cognitive science has taken on a novel twist from the use of another analog, the brain.[15]

It is worth underlining what Thagard calls 'the central hypothesis of cognitive science' – 'that thinking can best be understood in terms of representational structures in the mind and computational procedures that operate on those structures'. Phrased differently, he is saying *that cognitive science's most central concern has to do with the mental work involved in the storage and retrieval of experiences.* This central concern has, however, produced numbers of conflicting answers to questions about the nature of the representations and computations that make up thinking. Were there no debate about these, or were there complete certainty about the various structures, processes and so on involved in thinking, or the relationship between the brain and the mind, formulating a number of guidelines for teachers would have been relatively easy. As things stand, however, deciding on *what* to emphasise about cognitive science, or cognition as a field of study for educational purposes (as I advocate), demands another approach.

Answers to questions about what the mind contains (e.g. logical propositions, rules, concepts, images, and analogies), and how it operates (e.g. through deduction, search, matching, rotating, and retrieval) are already riddled with disagreements and dissent. When the brain is added to the mind-computer analogy, the study of cognition becomes a minefield.[16] The question is: why insist, as I do, on introducing the study of cognition to the curriculum of teachers?

Apart from thinking that cognitive science is the most suitable knowledge base for the task of *teaching* so as to ensure *learning* (in the process of transmitting a specific subject matter, of course), I think it is in confronting the disagreements, dissent, or minefield that teachers' knowledge will be enriched. In addition, the approach I take in this chapter will prevent teachers from using this

---

[15] http://plato.stanford.edu/entries/cognitive-science/ .

[16] It is salutary to remind ourselves of Fodor's statement that 'nothing at all is known about the laws according to which cognition supervenes on brain structures, or even about which brain structures it is that cognition supervenes on'; Fodor, J.A., *The Mind Doesn't Work That Way. The Scope and Limits of Computational Psychology* (Cambridge, MA: The MIT Press, 2001), 89.

or that favoured or current idea 'in the classroom' (as pointed out in the previous chapter regarding Piaget's and Vygotsky's work). More positively, confronting the disagreements, etc. will motivate teachers to turn ideas from cognitive science into hypotheses for and about education. This will not only refine what is known about cognition, but also create a worthy discipline around learning (and teaching): *applied cognition*.[17]

We also note in Thagard's summary[18] a particular emphasis on *cognitive architecture*, i.e. 'representational structures in the mind', and the manner in which *the mind works* to produce cognition, i.e. 'the computational procedures that operate on (the representational) structures'.[19] These two issues – the structures involved in learning, thinking, perception, memory, and knowing; and *how* cognition, as an organ or some kind of system, functions – are central to many debates about cognition. The question about *what* cognition is made up of (brain, mind, and perhaps more), is addressed by Andy Clark[20] in his outline of cognition, then and now.

Clark sketches progress in the study of cognition in terms of the following stages: (1) classical cognitivism, in which the mind was depicted in terms of 'a central logic engine, symbolic databases, and some peripheral "sensory" modules'; (2) a connectionist or artificial neural network approach, emphasising: (a) memory as pattern re-creation (rather than retrieval from a stored database), (b) problem-solving as pattern completion and pattern transformation (rather than as logical inference), and (c) a decentralised view of cognition (moving away from understanding cognition as involving a central processor); and finally (3) the view of the extended mind that Clark advocates. This view maintains connectionist ideas about memory, problem-solving and decentralisation, but

---

[17] See Ansari, D. and Coch, D., 'Bridges over troubled waters: Education and cognitive neuroscience', *Trends in Cognitive Sciences*, 10/4 (2006), 146–51, for an excellent example of the kind of work I have in mind.
[18] Thagard, 'Cognitive Science'.
[19] *Idem*.
[20] Clark, A., *Being There. Putting Brain, Body, and World Together Again* (Cambridge, MA: The MIT Press, 1999), 83–4.

augments this with two new tenets: first, that the environment is an active resource, whose intrinsic dynamics can play important problem-solving roles; and second, that the body is part of the computational loop.

The phases in the study of cognition over time, outlined above, are further unpacked below. In the rest of this section, I pay attention to classical cognitivism, distributed and embodied cognition, the brain, and further issues, positions and theories on what the study of cognition entails.

Classical cognitivism

Piaget stands out as the thinker who placed mind – as the seat of cognition, and the further reaches of this, knowledge[21] – on the *psychological* map. Like Chomsky, he too was concerned with modelling the inner workings of the mind. Both Piaget and Chomsky could be called competence theorists,[22] and both had quite a bit to say about what is innate,[23] even though they also disagreed on many things.[24]

The nativism of Chomsky specifies something about what the speaker/hearer of a language has to *know* prior to learning in order to construct a *theory* of language that correctly expresses the language's grammatical knowledge. It is further interesting to note that the nativism of Chomsky is neutral on evolution's role in shaping linguistic (in his case) competence.[25]

---

[21] Cf. Kitchener, R.F., *Piaget's* Theory of Knowledge. *Genetic Epistemology and Scientific Reason* (New Haven: Yale University Press, 1986).

[22] Cf. Pylyshyn, Z., 'The role of competence theories in cognitive psychology', *The Journal of Psycholinguistics*, 2/1 (1973), 21–50.

[23] Fodor writes that, 'The present phase of nativistic theorizing about the cognitive mind began with two suggestions of Noam Chomsky's: that there are substantive, universal constraints on the kinds of grammars that natural languages can have; and that these constraints express correspondingly substantive and universal properties of human psychology'; Fodor, *The Mind Doesn't Work That Way*, 9.

[24] Cf. Piatelli-Palmarini, M., *Language and Learning. The Debate between Jean Piaget and Noam Chomsky* (London: Routledge and Kegan Paul, 1980).

[25] Fodor draws the distinction between a basic rationalist epistemology and a rationalist psychology, or different kinds of nativism, as follows: '... whereas Chomsky's rationalism consists primarily in nativism about the knowledge that cognitive capacities manifest, New Synthesis rationalism consists primarily in nativism about the computational mechanisms that exploit such knowledge

60

Piaget, again, sees in the child's construction of reality (or changing psycho-logic) a repeat of the stages in the (historical) development of logico-mathematical (or scientific) thought. In psychological studies, Piaget's model of mind was given further shape and content in the work of Pascual-Leone.[26] Pascual-Leone's work is interesting in that he specifically attempted in his 'Theory of Constructive Operators' (TCO) to explicate the mechanisms involved in development.[27] Piagetian models of cognition, attempting (as they do) to resolve the gap between empiricist notions and rationalist theses regarding what we bring to the learning situation, are again taken up in the next chapter. Here, these models are used to underline a central characteristic of classical cognitivism: a concern with the inner, mental structures that generate manifest performance such as speech and cognition. This way of thinking about cognition started to change after Turing's ideas about formal, machine rationality. In Andy Clark's words, modelling cognition then started to consider 'the many and various ways body, brain and world interact so as to support fast, fluent responses in ecologically normal settings'.[28]

Distributed cognition

'Distributed cognition' as a model of cognition (and in some ways a kind of 'movement') was inaugurated by Hutchins and his colleagues in the '80s, and his now-famous book still inspires much of this kind of thinking.[29] Generally, in

---

for the purposes of cognition. To put it in a nutshell: *What's new about the New Synthesis is mostly the consequence of conjoining a rationalist epistemology with a syntactic notion of mental computation*; Fodor, *The Mind Doesn't Work That Way*, 12.
[26] Pascual-Leone, J., 'Vygotsky, Piaget, and the problem of Plato', *Swiss Journal of Psychology*, 55/2/3 (1996), 84–92; and Pascual-Leone, J., 'Organism processes for neo-Piagetian theories: A dialectical causal account of cognitive development', *International Journal of Psychology*, 22 (1987), 531–70.
[27] Cf. Pascual-Leone, J. and Goodman, D., *Intelligence and Experience: A Neo-Piagetian Approach. Report No. 81* (York, Ontario: York University, Department of Psychology, June 1979).
[28] Clark, A., 'Reasons, robots and the extended mind', *Mind and Language*, 16/2 (March 2001), 123.
[29] Hutchins, E., *Cognition in the Wild* (Cambridge, MA: The MIT Press, 1995).

distributed cognition terms, cognition is seen as a real-time *situated* activity that involves the brain and body (and its sensorimotor processes) – in cooperation with what is available in the environment. The central point of this view of cognition is that the props, tools and scaffolding *outside* the skin and skull *augment* the brain and other bodily functions and processes, in fact carrying some of the computational load. Clark asks in this regard:

> Instead of generating and updating a detailed inner model of the world, why not allow the world itself to 'store' the information, and retrieve what we need when we need it, by intelligent perception? In a certain light, the step of positing an inner world model intervening between perception and action thus seems absolutely spurious.[30]

He thus proposes, along Gibsonian lines, that we directly[31] perceive the world as a complex of possibilities for action.[32] 'We do not first represent the presence of a chair and then compute or infer its suitability for sitting; instead, to perceive a chair is, at one and the same time, to detect the opportunity for sitting.'[33] He puts this in an evolutionary perspective elsewhere in terms of a continuum between 'adaptive hookup' (as in a sunflower or light-seeking robot), and 'genuine internal representation as the hookup's complexity and systematicity increase' (in the case of creatures that engage in 'complex imaginings, off-line reflection, and counterfactual reasoning');[34] that is to say, creatures like us who engage, at times, in what I refer to below as 'higher' cognition.

[30] Clark, A., 'Moving minds: Situated content in the service of real-time success', *Philosophical Perspectives*, 9 (1995), 94.
[31] Cf. Gibson, J.J., 'The theory of affordances', in Shaw, R. and Bransford, J. (eds.), *Perceiving, Acting and Knowing: Towards an Ecological Psychology* (New Jersey: Lawrence Erlbaum Associates, Inc., 1977); and Rowlands, M., *The Body in Mind. Understanding Cognitive Processes* (Cambridge: CUP, 1999).
[32] Cf. Millikan, R.G., 'Pushmi-pullyu representations', *Philosophical Perspectives*, 9 (1995), 185–200.
[33] Clark, 'Moving minds', 95.
[34] Clark, *Being There*, 147.

Thus, a distributed view of cognition,[35] often in tandem with a focus on 'embodied cognition',[36] highlights the way we are placed or situated among other objects, things and people – bodily in a world – and how these are involved in cognition and problem-solving.[37] As Andy Clark puts it:

> It is a mistake to posit a biologically fixed 'human nature' with a simple 'wrap-around' of tools and culture. For the tools and culture are indeed as much determinants of our nature as products of it. Ours are (by nature) unusually plastic brains whose biologically proper functioning has always involved the recruitment and exploitation of non-biological props and scaffolds. More so than any other creature on the planet, we humans are *natural-born cyborgs*, factory tweaked and primed so as to participate in cognitive and computational architectures whose bounds far exceed those of skin and skull.[38]

These are seductive words, more so for education than simply as a statement about us (or how cognition is possible and how it works). I say this because whether problem-solving is *in truth* better conceived along distributed lines is both a matter of debate and open to ongoing empirical scrutiny. As a set of hypotheses for education, however, the distributed view of cognition offers interesting possibilities. We take this up again in the final chapter.

A distributed view of cognition is often associated with a specific focus on the body and its readiness to act in its world; for example, in the works of Thelen and Smith.[39] In this approach, the body is regarded as capable without being 'steered' as it were by a central executive. I separate the distributed and embodied

---

[35] Cf. http://eclectic.ss.uci.edu/~drwhite/Anthro179a/DistributedCognition.pdf .

[36] Cf. http://www.cogs.susx.ac.uk/users/ronc/papers/embodiment.pdf .

[37] For this, Clark coins the term 'wideware' (in addition to the brain, or wetware, and 'mind' or 'genetic algorithms' or software), to show how software, wetware and wideware form a deeply inter-animated triad. 'Wideware' refers to 'states, structures or processes that satisfy two conditions. First, the item in question must be in some intuitive sense environmental: it must not, at any rate, be realized within the biological brain or the central nervous system. ... Second, the item (state, structure, process) must play a functional role as part of an extended cognitive process: a process geared to the promotion of adaptation success via the gathering and use of knowledge and information, and one that loops out in some non-trivial way, so as to include and exploit aspects of the local bodily and environmental setting'; Clark, A., 'Where brain, body, and world collide', *Cognitive Systems Research*, 1/1 (1999), 5–17.

[38] Clark, 'Reasons, robots and the extended mind', 138.

[39] Thelen, E., and Smith, L., *A Dynamic Systems Approach to the Development of Cognition in Action* (Cambridge, MA: The MIT Press, 1994).

emphases for the sake of clarity and because I do not think that they necessarily go together; in the work of those just mentioned, however, the two emphases tend to blend together seamlessly. Nevertheless, separating the distributed and embodied approaches to cognition is useful for highlighting specific issues for the study of cognition.[40] For example, the distributed view emphasises what an environment offers cognition, while the embodied view highlights the body's capabilities. After discussing embodied cognition below, I draw the two emphases together to highlight particular problems for applied cognition.

Embodied cognition

The older, phenomenological study of perception by Merleau-Ponty,[41] shows in fine detail how the body is not merely some addition to cognition. He outlined how everything from the opposable thumb to the placement of our eyes, ears and so on, creates a perceptual horizon or meaningful perspective on things. Intuitively this makes sense, that is to say, anyone who has ever had to deal with disruptions in her normal sensory or active relationship to and in the world will appreciate the manner in which our bodiliness is not a negligible part of our thinking and acting. Thus, underlining our embodied natures, as Clark does, is timely.[42]

How big a slice to give the body and its feedback loops is discussed in terms of the *'Thesis of Radical Embodied Cognition'*,[43] about which Clark is circumspect. He prefers a view that places the brain at home in its proper bodily,

[40] Cf. Clark, A., 'An embodied cognitive science', *Trends in Cognitive Science*, 3/9 (September, 1999), 345–51; and http://www.cogs.susx.ac.uk/users/ronc/papers/embodiment.pdf.
[41] See Merleau-Ponty, M., *Phenomenology of Perception*, trans. R.C. McCleary (New York: Routledge and Kegan Paul, 1965).
[42] See Clark, 'Reasons, robots and the extended mind', 123; Clark, 'An embodied cognitive science';
http://www.cogs.susx.ac.uk/users/ronc/papers/embodiment.pdf ; and Clark, A., *Natural-born Cyborgs. Minds, Technologies, and the Future of Human Intelligence* (Oxford: OUP, 2003).
[43] Ibid., 148. Cf. Beer, R.D., 'Dynamical approaches to cognitive science', *Trends in Cognitive Science*, 4/3 (March 2000), 91–9; and Clark, A., 'The dynamical challenge', *Cognitive Science*, 21/4 (1997), 461–81.

cultural and environmental niche, because he thinks that this way makes things theoretically simpler than most mental representational views make them out to be.

In Clark's more recent work, he invites readers to 'allow our thoughts to go where no animal thoughts have gone before' courtesy of taking hold of our natural cyborg natures.[44] In this, Clark certainly challenges our common sense about the body – what it is and what it can do. Note how the metal-flesh interaction of the cyborg is both the stuff of science fiction and central to Clark's vision that this kind of interaction is *natural*. He writes:

> The cyborg is a potent cultural icon of the late twentieth century. It conjures images of human-machine hybrids and the physical merging of flesh and electronic circuitry. My goal is to hijack that image and to reshape it, revealing it as a disguised vision of (oddly) our own biological nature. For what is special about human brains, and what best explains the distinctive features of human intelligence, is precisely their ability to enter into deep and complex relationships with nonbiological constructs, props, and aids. This ability, however, does not depend on physical wire-and-implant mergers, so much as on our openness to information-processing mergers. Such mergers may be consummated without the intrusion of silicon and wire into flesh and blood, as anyone who has felt himself thinking via the act of writing already knows. The familiar theme of 'man the toolmaker' is thus taken one crucial step farther. Many of our tools are not just external props and aids, but they are deep and integral parts of the problem-solving systems we now identify as human intelligence. Such tools are best conceived as proper parts of the computational apparatus that constitutes our minds.[45]

What is particularly noteworthy in the above is the manner in which Clark's view both emphasises the physical structures involved in cognition (brain, body, and exosomatic scaffolding and props) *and* manages to turn cognition into a worldly-affair. A worldly-affair in which memory, or the representations of experiences, is 'action-orientated' rather than merely a set of stored information in the organism (brain).[46] That is to say, gone are the Cartesian and Kantian subjects, the brain as

---

[44] Clark, *Natural-born Cyborgs*, 198.
[45] *Ibid.*, 5–6.
[46] Cf. Clark, 'Where brain, body, and world collide', 5–17.

all-knowing central organiser, and the Rodin-like thinker, isolated from others and the world. These are replaced by an image of the busy animal, busy exploiting the wherewithal of its natural context. In this view, an animal does not have to *know* (somewhere in an 'inner' chamber) many things *before* acting, but *can do* a great many things *through* acting. This makes cognition indeed an embodied ability, a bit like the fly's ability to fly: 'All the fly has to do is jump off the wall, and the flapping [of wings] will follow'.[47]

On the face of it, showing how the body, brain, and world *together* act and solve problems seems to promise a concern with real, whole *people* and not (Piagetian) 'epistemic subjects' set up against the world 'out there'. The extended and embodied view of cognition thus seems to place us in a *context* of other people, things and especially language and culture. What is interesting about all this is that it has given renewed emphasis to the work of Vygotsky (and his ideas about the importance of social communication between people, to which we turn in the next chapter[48]). In addition, this view of cognition seems to side-step some of the more intractable problems in explaining aspects of cognition. For example, that new additions to the repertoire of the person – such as new habits, thoughts and skills – emerge, is taken for granted by the casual observer. In contrast, stage theories (like Piaget's) encountered 'the impossibility of acquiring "more powerful structures"' as an ongoing, logical difficulty in their theorising.[49]

This situated, embodied model of cognition also claims a better explanation for real-time, on-line problem-solving. This is a result of two shifts: first, positing less 'inside' the organism – which means that theories do not have to explicate an infinite set of executive functions to deliver the products of thinking efficiently; and second, attending more to the resources available

[47] Clark, 'Reasons, robots and the extended mind', 30.
[48] Vygotsky, L.S., *Mind in Society. The Development of Higher Psychological Processes*, Cole, M., John-Steiner, V., Scribner, S. and Souberman, E. (eds.) (Cambridge, MA: Harvard University Press, 1978).
[49] Cf. Piatelli-Palmarini, *Language and Learning*, 142–62; and Fodor, J.A., *The Language of Thought* (Cambridge, MA: Harvard University Press, 1970).

66

'outside' the mind/brain (e.g. various props and scaffolding in the world), and between organisms (e.g. sensitive feedback mechanisms).[50] Further, a distributed view of cognition has the advantage of allowing us to make sense of the facts of cognitive and epistemic (scientific) changes unequalled by (or unaccompanied by) similar brain and biological changes. This is possible because the attention has shifted to how the world (or what is outside the biological skin bag) comes to 'transform the problems posed to individual brains.'[51] In this regard, Hutchins's extensive and interesting work on a 'remembering' environment is indeed interesting.[52]

Before educators buy holus-bolus into these admittedly attractive notions related to a distributed and embodied model of cognition, a word of warning. We have to think more clearly about at least two problems: (1) Different *kinds* of things (say, books, PDAs, dictaphones, brains, human senses and other technological recorders of stimuli) operate according to different kinds of laws. For example, books don't forget, PDAs and dictaphones break when dropped, and human senses do not record everything that actually passes before them;[53] and (2) if one *kind* of thing is to find another kind useful or resourceful, mechanisms for coordination between the two are essential. Consider the case of a book containing relevant information that a person requires. Unless the person can decipher the code in which the information is stored, the book is useless. The problem-solver (animal or machine, metal or flesh) has to have certain links[54] to the resources *outside* of its own 'skin bag' if these are to count as resources. These

---

[50] Cf. Clark, *Being There* – particularly the discussion on 11–69.
[51] *Ibid.*, 66.
[52] Hutchins, *Cognition in the Wild*.
[53] As Nietszche observed: to a purely cognitive being, knowledge would be a matter of indifference; and I want to say that to a technological recording device, *what* it records is of no interest; but in trying to explain what a person sees, etc. the theorist has to include interest, attention, and so on.
[54] Cf. the general excitement about the discovery of 'mirror neurons':
http://arjournals.annualreviews.org/doi/abs/10.1146/annurev.neuro.27.070203.144230 .
http://www.brainconnection.com/content/181_1 and Carpendale, J.I.M. and Lewis, C., 'Constructing an understanding of mind: The development of children's social understanding within social interaction', *Behavioral and Brain Sciences*, 27 (2004), 79–151.

links can be something as commonplace as the ability to read script, or they can be more fascinating parts of our neural equipment, such as the ability to 'read' the emotions and intentions of another.

These two problems at least question whether cognition now has all the answers. For example, are we really rid of the Captain steering things (a central processing or executive function) when it comes to higher cognition? Moreover, do the collection of tricks and strategies (e.g. pattern recognition), coupled with feedback loops, and operating according to a parallel computational system suffice to explain and guide all cognitive activity? These are empirical questions and time and more research will tell.

We will encounter further difficulties in outlining what cognition is all about below; but first we consider other parts of cognitive architecture.

The study of the brain

Few would not agree that the brain is central to cognition, but to include the study of the brain in the curriculum of teachers might be more controversial. For decades, psychology and certainly education too have gone on with their merry business of intervening in people's lives without as much as a thought for the brain and body. This seems no longer tenable.

For those who want to harness the brain and its capabilities for education, there is an increasing body of research to rely on.[55] For example, when we consider that learning is not only made possible by various cortical structures, but that learning itself may change the brain structures,[56] applied cognition cannot

---

[55] See Ansari and Coch, 'Bridges over troubled waters: Education and cognitive neuroscience'.

[56] Cf. Anderson, M., 'Ask not what you can do for modularity but what can modularity do for you', *Learning and Individual Differences*, 10/3 (1998), 251–7; Karmiloff-Smith, A., 'Development itself is the key to understanding developmental disorders', *Trends in Cognitive Science*, 2/10 (1998), 389–98; Quartz, S.R., 'The constructivist brain', *Trends in Cognitive Science*, 3/2 (1999), 48–57; Quartz, S.R. and Sejnowski, T.J., 'The neural basis of cognitive development: A constructivist manifesto', *Behavioral and Brain Sciences*, 20 (1997), 537–96; and

avoid the study of the brain and its structures, functions, and their relationship to what happens in the classroom. Further, when noting that learning may 'set' the brain from the process of myelination[57] through to what happens synaptically,[58] in one rather than another way, the brain becomes a crucial topic or focal point in the study of cognition. At the very least, educators may concern themselves with whether the brains before them had enough nutrients to develop optimally and are thus in a good condition.[59] And, if the eliminative materialism[60] of Paul Churchland,[61] for example, is found to explain everything we now include under

---

Thomas, M., 'Quo vadis modularity in the 1990s', *Learning and Individual Differences*, 10/3 (1998), 245–50.

[57] 'During the first months of life there is a massive increase in the cortex in the insulating substance myelin ... Once the axon is insulated with myelin, it conducts the electrical signal far more efficiently. Clearly, a movement as delicate as voluntary reaching can only occur when the neurons in the cortex are working as efficiently as possible. Myelination continues apace right up to fifteen years of age, and even beyond. Furthermore, it is a pleasing thought that myelein can even continue to increase in density to as late in life as sixty years of age.' Greenfield, S. *The Human Brain. A Guided Tour* (London: Phoenix, 1997), 132.

[58] 'You are your synapses', as LeDoux puts the bottom line of his book: LeDoux, J., *Synaptic Self. How Our Brains Become Who We Are* (London, Penguin, 2002), ix.

[59] Cf. Greenfield, *The Human Brain*.

[60] 'Eliminative materialism (EM) is the conjunction of two claims. First, our common sense "belief-desire" conception of mental events and processes, our "folk psychology", is a false and misleading account of the causes of human behavior. Second, like other false conceptual frameworks from both folk theory and the history of science, it will be replaced by, rather than smoothly reduced or incorporated into, a future neuroscience. Folk psychology is the collection of common homilies about the causes of human behavior. You ask me why Marica is not accompanying me this evening. I reply that her grant deadline is looming. You nod sympathetically. You understand my explanation because you share with me a generalization that relates beliefs about looming deadlines, desires about meeting professionally and financially significant ones, and ensuing free-time behavior. It is the collection of these kinds of homilies that EM claims to be flawed beyond significant revision. Although this example involves only beliefs and desires, folk psychology contains an extensive repertoire of propositional attitudes in its explanatory nexus: hopes, intentions, fears, imaginings, and more. To the extent that scientific psychology (and neuroscience!) retains folk concepts, EM applies to it as well. EM is physicalist in the classical sense, postulating some future brain science as the ultimately correct account of (human) behavior. It is eliminative in predicting the future removal of folk psychological kinds from our post-neuroscientific ontology'; Bickle, J. and Mandik, P., 'The philosophy of neuroscience', in Zalta, E.N. (ed.), *The Stanford Encyclopedia of Philosophy* (Winter 2002 Edition), URL = <http://plato.stanford.edu/archives/win2002/entries/neuroscience/> .

[61] Churchland, P.M., *The Engine of Reason, the Seat of the Soul. A Philosophical Journey into the Brain* (Cambridge, MA: The MIT Press, 2000).

reasoning and rationality, then the brain becomes the main topic to be included in the study of cognition.[62]

The brain as a part of what is involved in cognition, perhaps even a central part, takes the study of cognition into biology, in general. In addition, focusing on the brain, body and biology, highlights questions about what is innate, i.e. what the learner brings to a task *prior* to learning. In recent times, this is a central concern of those involved in one or the other branch of evolutionary studies; for example, in discussions about (natural or evolved) differences in the male and female brains that are said to be responsible for differences in performance of various much valued skills, technology and knowledge.[63]

As we saw above in our discussion of the study of cognition now, the distributed and embodied views on cognition turn our attention to our brains, bodies and biological natures. In addition, the prominence of debates around, for example, 'cloning' (as the popular media have dubbed the more serious business of stem cell research[64]) certainly place our evolutionary history and the way this is thought to influence our natures on everyone's lips.[65] It is thus time that education too took note.

---

[62] See the following discussion of the neuronal basis of what makes us as we are: 'What I know depends on the specific configuration of connections among my trillion neurons, on the neurochemical interactions between connected neurons, and on the response portfolio of different neuron types. All this is what makes me me'; Churchland, P.S., 'How do neurons know?', *Daedalus*, Winter 2004, 1, URL = <http://findarticles.com/p/articles/mi_qa3671/is_200401/ai_n9380531>.

[63] Cf. the various responses to the speech by Lawrence Summers (president of Harvard) in January 2005 regarding the natural differences between men and women, which apparently explain the under-representation of women in science and engineering; e.g. Walter, N., 'Prejudice and evolution', *Prospect* (June 2005), 35; Wolcott, J., 'Caution: Women seething', *Vanity Fair* (June 2005), 64; and Silverman, I. and Eals, M., 'Sex differences in spatial abilities: Evolutionary theory and data', in Barkow, J.H., Cosmides, L., and Tooby, J. (eds.), *The Adapted Mind. Evolutionary Psychology and the Generation of Culture* (Oxford: OUP, 1992), 533–53.

[64] Cf. http://www.ornl.gov/sci/techresources/Human_Genome/elsi/cloning.shtml#whatis ; http://www.roslin.ac.uk/public/cloning.html ; http://www.ornl.gov/sci/techresources/Human_Genome/home.shtml ; http://stemcells.nih.gov/index.asp .

[65] The Africa Genome Education Institute has recently added a booklet entitled 'Our Genes' to a popular weekly newspaper. Cf. www.africagenome.co.za .

70

In general, it is worth reminding ourselves that, even though Darwin's ideas have been around for a century and a half it is only recently that the social sciences have begun to take on evolution. The important issue for our discussion is whether (and if so, to what degree) evolution has something to say about cognition.[66] It seems to me that it has, in particular by way of answers to questions about human nature, innate knowledge, prepared learning, and intelligence as a *product* of evolution. Moreover, our (evolved) intelligence produces, in its turn, other human products such as culture; the latter which certainly plays a big part in learning and the differences between us.[67]

I thus think that Pinker is right to take on the 'Blank Slate', the 'Noble Savage', and the 'Ghost in the Machine' as certain blocks to looking at *human nature* more clearly.[68] I also think that he is right in arguing that these are used to soften the blows about differences between us, and seemingly universal – mostly nasty – inclinations that also mark our species. I leave these at that.[69]

I do not, however, see the theory of evolution as a panacea for all our questions, or expect it to heal the rift between the natural and social or human sciences as Plotkin[70] and Wilson[71] want it to. We, like all animals, have evolved

---

[66] Consider the following war cry in this regard by Millikan: 'Reasoning, I insist, is done in the world, not in one's head. Logical possibility (known *a priori*) is impossible. And the only hope for intentional psychology is to embrace its biological roots'; and Millikan, R.G., *White Queen Psychology and Other Essays for Alice* (Cambridge, MA: The MIT Press, 1995), 12.
[67] Craig, A.P., 'The study of change', in *Cognitive Development in Southern Africa*, compiled by H van Niekerk (Pretoria: Human Sciences Research Council, 1991); Craig, A.P., 'Adult cognition and tertiary studies', *South African Journal of Higher Education*, 5/2 (1991), 137–44; and Craig, A.P., 'A cognitive infrastructure for change', *Theoria*, LXX (1987), 77–83.
[68] Pinker, S., *The Blank Slate* (London: Penguin, 2002), 1–58 – but really throughout this work.
[69] It is however worth noting in passing that even if the worst comes to the worst and definitive data on, say, women's *genetic* limitations regarding one or the other desirable or social valued skills come forward, this still leaves various *practical* questions open (moral, political and educational). That is to say, there are a number of obvious examples around which to build arguments *against* thinking of genetic factors as the only limitations in deciding what to do and how to live. An obvious example is when two healthy, fertile, sexually active people – i.e. those who are intrinsically 'favoured' in terms of reproduction and sex – decide whether to procreate at all, or how many children to produce, and how to manage their individual sexual desires in the name of a commitment to a life-long, monogamous union.
[70] Plotkin, H., *The Imagined World Made Real* (London: Penguin, 2003).
[71] Wilson, E.O., *Consilience. The Unity of Knowledge* (London: Abacus, 1998).

tendencies that must be acknowledged. Thus, I also do not think it productive to avoid the implications of this, as some of those on the political left and moral right wing[72] seem to do. Generally speaking, it is clear that there are many empirical questions about human nature, in particular about what we bring to the learning situation, as well as a great deal of theorising still to be done before closing the book on the biological side to our lives.

Getting a clearer grip on biological constraints on learning, for example, alerts us to the possibility that there might be things that *cannot* be learned (e.g. to un-see certain well-known illusions such as the Mueller-Lyer figures[73]); and, in addition, the possibility that much of perception, at least on the local, stupid side of it,[74] might be closed to learning in the traditional 'instructive' sense[75] of this term. If both of these are correct, applied cognition might have to privilege a view of learning, in the instructive sense of this, as involving primarily the so-called higher cognitions (thinking and problem-solving).[76]

At the one extreme, therefore, the biological sciences underline the possibility that there is nothing to do about learning (or unlearning) in the traditional 'instructive' sense[77] when dealing with 'hardwired' responses – even though interesting empirical questions do exist with respect to establishing what school tasks, or parts of these, fall into categories like the illusions. At the other

---

[72] Cf. Walter, N., 'Prejudice and evolution', *Prospect* (June 2005), 34–9.

[73] Fodor, J.A., *A Theory of Content and Other Essays* (Cambridge, MA: MIT Press, 2002), 198.

[74] 'If the perceptual mechanisms are indeed local, stupid, and extremely nervous, it is teleologically sensible to have the picture of the world that they present tempered, reanalysed, and – as Kant saw – above all integrated by slower, better informed, more conservative, and more holistic cognitive systems'; Fodor, *A Theory of Content and Other Essays*, 203.

[75] Cf. Piatelli-Palmarini, M., 'Evolution, selection and cognition: From "learning" to parameter setting in biology and in the study of language', *Cognition*, 31 (1989), 1–44.

[76] Fodor thinks that the perceptual mechanisms are encapsulated, and quite different from, the so-called higher cognition about which he writes, 'So little is known about them that one is hard-put even to say *which* true higher cognitive faculties there are. But "thought" and "problem-solving" are surely among the names in the game, and [he suggests] these are everything that perception is not: slow, deep, global rather than local, largely voluntary (or, as one says, "executive") control, typically associated with diffuse neurological structures, neither bottom-to-top nor top-to-bottom in their modes of processing, but characterized by computations in which information flows every which way. Above all, they are paradigmatically *un*encapsulated'; Fodor, *A Theory of Content and Other Essays*, 202.

[77] Cf. Piatelli-Palmarini, 'Evolution, selection and cognition'.

72

extreme, we are more or less certain that learning is possible, given our (biological) nature, and thus motivated to continue to attempt (through at least two participating agents, 'teacher', and 'pupil') to enrich, extend, and so forth, the background knowledge that allows for interpretation, thinking, and problem-solving. Such deliberate instruction is more often than not aimed at furnishing the learner with the requisite knowledge, say, through learning physics, with which to reshape the perceptual field[78] involved in thinking about very particular tasks.[79]

Further issues

For the sake of more completeness to the outline of relevant issues and foci in the study of cognition, it may be noted that there are other positions on cognition between the ones briefly indicated above. Some of these will be discussed in the next two chapters. They depend on, for example: (a) different epistemic assumptions (e.g. rationalism, empiricism, evolutionary epistemology); (b) different views on how experiences, memories, and stimuli, recorded through the senses, are stored (e.g. lingua-form, text-like, or picture-form representations, or as Turing-like syntactically structured representations); and (c) different conceptions of how the mind operates (e.g. mechanically[80]), and what it operates on (e.g. innate knowledge, or evolved modules[81] with specifiable

---

[78] Fodor, *A Theory of Content and Other Essays*, 259.
[79] Fodor writes that 'Thinking is hard' and like 'the processes of scientific discovery' – which are not only hard, but mysterious too; and one can only agree; Fodor, *A Theory of Content and Other Essays*, 216.
[80] 'It's a remarkable fact that you can tell, just by looking at it, that any (declarative) sentence of the syntactic form P and Q ("John swims and Mary drinks," for example) is true if and only if P and Q are themselves both true; that is, that sentences of the form P *and* Q, entail, and are entailed by, the corresponding sentences P, Q. To say that "you can tell this just by looking" is to claim that you don't have to know anything about what either P or Q *means* to see that these entailment relations hold, and that you also don't have to know anything about the nonlinguistic world.' ... 'This line of thought is often summarized by saying that some inferences are "formally valid", which is in turn to say that they hold just in virtue of the "syntax" of the sentences that enter into them. It was Turing's great discovery that machines can be designed to evaluate any inference that is formally valid in that sense ... So: Turing showed us how to make a computing machine that will recognize any argument that is valid in virtue of its syntax ...'; Fodor, *The Mind Doesn't Work That Way*, 12–3.
[81] Fodor, in *The Mind Doesn't Work That Way*, distinguishes, first, between those making a distinction between modules that imply informational encapsulation, and those that don't; the

content[82]). Then, too, different theorists give dissimilar weight to the causal efficacy of ordinary or folk psychological intentional and teleological talk, the import of which is unpacked below in terms of Fodor's questions about how the mind works.

At each turn, so to speak, the story about cognition looks different and the study of cognition involves different entities, processes and mechanisms. Moreover, it is important to remind ourselves of something that is at the heart of all this disagreement; i.e. our intuitions about 'brain' and 'mind', and their putative interrelationship and respective roles in the life of man.

Few would *not* admit to the brain being a physical organ, but what it does and how it does this is not all that clear or agreed upon. It looks so unlike a computer or any other form of 'hardware' that Clark's 'wetware'[83] is some attempt

---

former has to do with the 'usage according to which anything that is or purports to be a functionally individuated cognitive mechanism – anything that would have a proprietary box in a psychologist's information flow diagram – thereby counts as a module', and goes on to say that 'everybody who thinks that mental states have any sort of structure that's specifiable in functional terms qualifies as a modularity theorist in this diluted sense' (56). Then, second, there is the usage typical of Chomsky in which a module is simply a body of innate knowledge; and Chomskian modules are largely neutral about encapsulation and abduction. Then, the more tendentious usage combines 'domain specificity' (58), evolution and adaptionism, and a computational 'Theory of Mind' to get to something like the following: 'This means that there is a more or less encapsulated processor for each kind of problem that it can solve: and, in particular, that there is nothing in the mind that can ask questions about which solution to a problem is "best overall", that is, best in light of the totality of a creature's beliefs and utilities' (64); it is the latter he finds fault with.
[82] See Neander, K., 'Teleological theories of mental content', in Zalta, E.N. (ed.), *The Stanford Encyclopedia of Philosophy* (Summer 2004 Edition), URL = <http://plato.stanford.edu/archives/sum2004/entries/content-teleological/> . 'Teleological theories of mental content try to explain the contents of mental representations by appealing to a teleological notion of function. Take, for example, the thought that blossoms are forming. On a representational theory of thought, this thought involves a representation of blossoms forming, and a theory of content aims among other things to tell us why this representation has that content; it aims to say why it is a thought about blossoms forming rather than about the sun shining or pigs flying or nothing at all. In general, a theory of content tries to say why a mental representation counts as representing what it represents. According to teleological theories of content, what a representation represents depends on the functions of the systems that use or (it depends on the version) produce the representation. The relevant notion of function is said to be the one that is used in biology and neurobiology in attributing functions to components of organisms (as in "the function of the pineal gland is releasing melatonin" and "the function of brain area MT is processing information about motion"). Proponents of teleological theories of content generally understand this notion to be the notion of what something was selected for, either by ordinary natural selection or by some other natural process of selection.'
[83] See note 37, above.

to express something about the 'feel' of it.[84] Then, too, there are also debates about how to treat 'mind'. In this case, many would disagree that it is a real, physical organ. For some, 'mind' (1) is just another word for the brain (and a misleading one at that); (2) indicates another (other than physical/material) line of causation – it is thus a word for the causal properties of 'the mental' (e.g. desires and beliefs); (3) is a label for interesting, emergent properties of the brain (e.g. consciousness); or (4) is another kind of metaphysical entity. The latter is typical of Descartes's dualistic view of reality.

Moreover, decisions about the brain and mind involve various ontological commitments (to physicalism[85]), blunders (postulated things, entities, mechanisms, and processes that do not in fact exist), or deliberate attempts to clean things up.[86] I leave these debates to the professionals,[87] and turn to my last attempt to find clear boundary markers for the study of cognition without getting embroiled in the business of selling this or that theory, principle or fact about cognition to teachers.

3.2 Fodor's guided tour[88]

I rely on the work of Jerry Fodor because the questions he asks point to many of the debates that make the study of cognition confusing to newcomers. My purpose is to underline the way specific questions and answers *organise* thinking about cognition.

---

[84] As does the Monty Python depiction of the brain: 'The human brain is like an enormous fish. It's flat and slimy, and has gills through which it can see'; in 'Matching Tie & Handkerchief' LP http://www.intriguing.com/mp/_scripts/matchtie.asp .

[85] Cf. Churchland, *The Engine of Reason.*

[86] Cf. Ross, D. and Spurrett, D., 'What to say to a sceptical metaphysician: A defense manual for cognitive and behavioural scientists', *Behavioral and Brain Sciences*, 27/5 (2004), 603–27.

[87] Cf. Kim, J., *Supervenience and Mind* (Cambridge, MA: CUP, 1993); and Kim, J., 'Multiple realization and the metaphysics of reduction', *Philosophy and Phenomenological Research*, 52 (1992), 1–26.

[88] This is the section that Spurrett (in the Preface) questioned most; Fodor himself (in an email response to the author) was not sure that questions and issues such as those introduced here would offer the enterprise of education anything. I, in turn, think that this section is crucial as an outline of the different – and often confusing – positions in the study of cognition.

Fodor asks the following nested questions about *mental representations* – arguably the most crucial part of what cognition involves – in order to demonstrate agreements and disagreements between participants. These positions on the study of cognition are the results of differing hunches about the best options to pursue in the ontology game or what to think about mental and psychological things/states/processes.[89] The main questions are about propositional attitudes, the status of our ordinary explanations of actions, what is real, and truth-conditions. The different answers given to these by participants create, in effect, different positions and commitments in the study of cognition.

1. How do you feel about propositional attitudes?

'Propositional attitudes' have to do with intentional, common-sense psychological explanations.[90] That is to say, these are thought to account for voluntary behaviour by citing the beliefs and desires in view of which certain actions are undertaken, and defending the reasonableness and rightness of acting in light of these. The question being asked is: what is the status of these (ordinary) explanations?

The differing answers to this pan out as follows: a *realist* thinks that mental states cause behaviour, respects folk psychological generalisations in this regard, and holds that these causally efficacious mental states are open to assessment in terms of the truth/falseness of the beliefs in question and whether the desire was in fact fulfilled/frustrated. Opposed to this, *anti-realists* could be either of the instrumentalist kind (i.e. they permit talk about actions in terms of desires and beliefs – taking the intentional stance[91] – but do not literally subscribe to the ontological commitments of belief/desire psychology); or of the kind that

---

[89] I omit from what follows his fine rendering of the philosophy involved, and the various arguments for/against specific options on each.

[90] Cf. Taylor, C., *Human Agency and Language. Philosophical Papers 1* (Cambridge: CUP, 1992), 164–86, for a spirited defence of upholding 'in the general case the logic of our ordinary language of feeling, action and desire'.

[91] See Dennett, D.C., *Darwin's Dangerous Idea. Evolution and the Meanings of Life* (London: Penguin, 1995), 229–30; he distinguishes between the design, physical, and intentional stances. The latter has to do with trying to figure out what the designers of one or the other object had in mind, i.e. what they intended.

thinks belief/desire psychology is just a false theory or a case of bad science and that it ought thus to be got rid of. So, anti-realists are either instrumentalists, or not, which gets the non-instrumentalists to the next question.

2. *How do you feel about functionalism?*[92]

'Functionalism just is the doctrine that the psychologist's theoretical taxonomy doesn't need to look "natural" from the point of view of any lower-level science.'[93] How you feel about functionalism thus has to do with how comfortable you are with different levels of explanation, and perhaps incompatible hypotheses such as those simultaneously phrased in terms of common-sense belief/desire/psychology, neurological (or circuit-theoretic), hard science explanations, and something in between – the theories of (functionalist) cognitive scientists, for example. If functionalism[94] is true, it is these hybrid theories that are preserved.

So: 'If you think that there are beliefs and desires, and you think that they are functional states, then you get to answer the following diagnostic question'.[95]

3. *Are propositional attitudes monadic functional states?*

What itches here (or perhaps what philosophers scratch at, whether it itches or not) has to do with what is *really real* – the ultimate stuff. Answers to this involve contenders such as mental states (intentions, meaning), their relationships to one another, and the causal interrelations thus constituted. Phrased differently, the questions are about how a propositional attitude maps onto propositional content, and the causal links that thus make up mental states, processes and whatever else.

---

[92] See Levin, J., 'Functionalism', in Zalta, E.N. (ed.), *The Stanford Encyclopedia of Philosophy* (Fall 2004 Edition), URL = <http://plato.stanford.edu/archives/fall2004/entries/functionalism/> .
[93] Fodor, *A Theory of Content and Other Essays*, 10.
[94] 'It is usual to note that etiological (teleological) functions are distinct from the causal-role functions involved in what is called "functionalism" in philosophy of mind'; Neander, K., 'Teleological theories of mental content'.
[95] Fodor, *A Theory of Content and Other Essays*, 12.

The answers here (ignoring certain in-between positions to avoid muddying the waters) turn into two positions: answering 'no' produces an alignment to the Representational Theory of Mind (RTM), while a 'yes' gets you to what Fodor dubs 'Standard Realism' (SR for convenience). He clarifies this as follows:

> SR is a compound of two doctrines: a claim about the 'internal' structure of attitudes (viz., that they are monadic functional states) and a claim about the source of their semantical properties (viz. that some or all of such properties arise from isomorphisms between the causal role of mental states and the implicational structure of propositions).[96]

And:

> RTM assumes the heavier burden of ontological commitment. It quantifies not just over such mental states as believing that P and desiring that Q but also over mental representations; symbols in a 'language of thought'.[97]

What the RTM allows for is a grasp of mental processes (not only states), a theory of thinking, trains of thought and arguments. Thus, after Turing's insight was put to work making computers, the problem of mediating between causal properties of symbols and their semantic properties was solved, or so says Fodor. In his words:

> The trick is to abandon associationism[98] and combine RTM with the 'computer metaphor'. In this respect I think there really has been something like an intellectual breakthrough. Technical details to one side, this is – in my view – the only respect in which contemporary Cognitive Science represents a major advance over the versions of RTM that were its eighteenth- and nineteenth-century predecessors.[99]

The last question has to do with the semantic story RTM has to tell if it 'is going to be Realist about the attitudes and the attitudes have their propositional objects essentially'.[100]

---

[96] *Ibid.*, 15–16.
[97] *Ibid.*, 16.
[98] Being a realist about attitudes requires something other than associationism to produce a credible mechanism for thinking.
[99] *Ibid.*, 22.
[100] *Ibid.*, 25.

4. How do you feel about truth-conditions?

One story to tell, concerning functional-role (FR) semantics,[101] goes something like this:

> 'Believing, desiring, and so forth are relations between intentional systems and mental representations that get tokened (in their heads, as it might be). Tokening a mental representation has causal consequences. The totality of such consequences implies a network of causal interrelations among the attitudes ...' and so on to a functional-role semantics.[102]

There is, however,

> ... no unique best mapping of the causal roles of mental states on to the inferential network of propositions or [...] even if there is, such a mapping would nevertheless underdetermine assignments of contents to attitudes.[103]

FR semantics therefore does not really get its causes and propositions in convincing order, nor does it have enough to say about the mind-to-world problem to satisfy naturalistic scruples about the semantic and intentional in the natural order. This means, at least, that there is more work to be done in answering the question about whether there is anything besides prejudice that underwrites our common-sense psychological intuitions about the relationship between the meanings things have for us, and the causes of thoughts and actions.

---

[101] 'Developing and defending theories of content is a central topic in current philosophy of mind. A common desideratum in this debate is a theory of cognitive representation consistent with a physical or naturalistic ontology. ... When one perceives or remembers that he is out of coffee, his brain state possesses intentionality or "aboutness." The percept or memory is about one's being out of coffee; it represents one as being out of coffee. The representational state has content. A psychosemantic seeks to explain what it is for a representational state to be about something: to provide an account of how states and events can have specific representational content. A physicalist psychosemantic seeks to do this by using resources of the physical sciences exclusively. Neurophilosophers have contributed to two types of physicalist psychosemantics: the Functional Role approach and the Informational approach. The core claim of functional role semantics holds that a representation has its content in virtue of relations it bears to other representations. ... The neurobiological paradigm for informational semantics is the *feature detector*: one or more neurons that are (i) maximally responsive to a particular type of stimulus, and (ii) have the function of indicating the presence of that stimulus type. Examples of such stimulus-types for visual feature detectors include high-contrast edges, motion direction, and colors. A favorite feature detector among philosophers is the alleged fly detector in the frog'; Bickle and Mandik, 'The philosophy of neuroscience'.

[102] *Idem.*

[103] *Idem.*

It may be that what one descries, just there on the farthest horizon, is a glimpse of a causal/teleological theory of meaning … and it may be that the development of such a theory would provide a way out of the current mess.[104]

Fodor's hope for getting us out of the current mess is indeed some way of focusing the agreements and disagreements around mental representations he outlines – debates that bring to the fore a variety of specific issues, positions and theories in the study of cognition; for example, issues such as the status of our everyday causal explanations, positions such as realists versus anti-realists, and theories such as the RTM.

We may also note that two primary worries run throughout the debates: (a) the *ontological* status of: mental states, mental processes, the contents of thought, trains of thought and arguments (involving stating premises, drawing inferences, and reaching a conclusion), and other crucial characteristics of our mental lives or cognition, and (b) the *causal* status of the reasons we give for our actions, or the relationship between common-sense belief/desire/psychology, and neurological or circuit-theoretic, hard scientific explanations.

One more issue in the study of cognition deserves an airing in this chapter: the meaning of 'higher' cognition.

3.3 Higher cognition

This distinction between high and low cognition is not often encountered in the literature on the distributed and embodied models discussed above. Outside of these, and for those worried by what Pascual-Leone called 'Plato's problem'[105] (we will discuss this in the next chapter), or the 'frame problem' in more recent writing,[106] the distinction is of considerable importance. Overcoming this problem

---

[104] *Ibid.*, 28.

[105] Pascual-Leone, 'Vygotsky, Piaget, and the problem of Plato', 84–96.

[106] Difficulties in solving the search, movement and update of information within a large body of stored quasi-linguistic encodings in (AI) systems; see Clark, 'Moving minds', 90.

emphasises the difference between practical and abstract intelligence, as well as of the difference between animal and mature human thought.[107] The latter involves, in particular, the 'combination of tool and sign in psychological activity' and thus the transformation of practical, animal intelligence into higher psychological functions.[108] The distinction between high and low cognition also clarifies the differences between an empiricist and rationalist view of mental states and processes (i.e. the contents of thought and the causal effects of having particular thoughts).[109] I therefore think the distinction crucial for the task at hand: determining what the study of cognition entails for education.

If cognition, without distinction, is something that *happens* all the way from the local, particular and automatic (dumb, reflex-like) responses to great and unique inventions, then we are indeed dealing with something the fly, the frog, the tuna, Rodney Brooks's machines[110] and all of us, have more or less of. This is not satisfying because, as such, 'cognition' includes too much. The more focused responses to stimuli that Einstein engaged in too require attention (his thinking on the train on his way to work, in the patent office where he worked, and on his long strolls on the outskirts of the city Bern with his friend, which finally saw the light of day as $L=MV^2$ in his publication of 1905[111]).

If we hold onto a picture of cognition as being without distinction, then teaching or education (in the sense of a deliberate focus on certain knowledge in specific ways), loses all ground to Nature. I am not particularly worried about us joining the company of other animals, even flies and other lowly creatures, but I do not think that Nature explains all cognition, because there is such an enormous

---

[107] Cf. Markman, A.B. and Gentner, D., 'Thinking', *Annual Review of Psychology*, 52 (2000), 223–47, for a helpful review of issues at stake; and Prasada, S., 'Acquiring generic knowledge', *Trends in Cognitive Science*, 4/2 (2000), 66–72, for a discussion of this in terms of acquiring knowledge of *kinds*.
[108] Vygotsky, *Mind in Society*, 52–7.
[109] Fodor, *A Theory of Content and Other Essays*, 20–21.
[110] http://people.csail.mit.edu/brooks/ .
[111] Bodanis, D., *E=MC². A Biography of the World's Most Famous Equation* (London: Macmillan, 2000), 7 and 326n8.

gap between the products and demands of different kinds of cognition; for example, between scientific *knowledge*, and what we and other animals do merely to get by from day to day,[112] and between *thinking*, and merely *acting* without thought. I thus want to motivate the study of specifically higher forms of cognition for the task at hand: improving on learning and teaching.

On the face of it, *some* people, *some* of the time, do something that ought to be called higher cognition; that is to say, engage in a *kind* of cognition that so far outstrips available data, information, experiences and existing skills, technology and knowledge that one wants to ask: how *does* the mind/brain, even the embodied and situated brain, do it? Moreover, one wants to ask about this kind of thinking in order to answer the question of whether education can harness enough of the relevant *cognitive architecture* (and the functions, processes, etc. involved) to produce better cognitive products and greater knowledge.

By way of concluding this chapter, allow me to highlight the following beacons in the study of cognition. The first beacon to highlight is *the mind* – what it is and how it operates, and its relationship to the body and world, or to biology and history. Then, we need to highlight *the brain,* what it is and does – i.e. its structures, functions, and development; the neurological constraints on learning; and the relationship of the brain to the mind and cognition. We also need to highlight particular *processes* involved in cognition – for example, learning, memory, perception – and certain *cognitive accomplishments* – such as novel inventions, scientific thinking, problem-solving. Lastly, we need to highlight how the study of these as well as an awareness of the various debates, positions and viewpoints on cognition can lead us in any one of a number of different directions in the study of cognition – a study aimed above all at making and testing productive hypotheses for improving learning and teaching.

---

[112] Cf. http://whyfiles.org/siegfried/story01/ .

CHAPTER 4

Evolution's Gift

In this chapter I want to pose 'learning' as a problem, and then subject it to conceptual scrutiny, because I believe this ordinary word, at home in everyday talk and common sense, leads us astray. This philosophical work suggests three hypotheses about the origin of knowledge for further, empirical scrutiny. After this, we turn to a theoretical framing of learning from the perspective of the study of cognition.

Pre-reflectively, 'learning' seems like an answer to a question about how a knowledge system (machine, animal, or group) acquires something new; for example, how a particular addition to a neophyte's habitual cognitive, emotional, volitional, or behavioural repertoire occurred. Yet, upon closer examination, 'learning' is not so much an *explanation* for acquiring something new, as a name for a problem.[1]

That something like 'learning' occurs seems obvious enough. We notice it in individual lives and historically – 'learning', meaning here, more or less: doing, thinking, or knowing something *new*, something not clearly just part of our natures or what we were born with. How to account for all this, or the emergence of the new, is not all that easy though.

For one thing: what is the source or origin of the new acquisition? For another, how do we give appropriate weight to, for example, the relative

---

[1] Cf. http://findarticles.com/p/articles/mi_qa3671/is_200401 for articles by Howard Gardner, Jerome Bruner, Michael Tomasello, Patricia Smith Churchland, and others on learning.

84

contributions of: maturation, development and learning – if these are indeed different processes involving different structures? Making distinctions such as these alerts us to the possible role of perspective on what is observed, or our particular theoretical orientation to learning.[2] For example, *development* is the focus of Piaget's work[3] and *learning* that of Vygotsky's,[4] and considering the relationship between development and learning brings to the fore the older opposition between 'nature' and 'nurture'[5] (made famous by Francis Galton)[6] – an opposition possibly also at work in the gap between seemingly universal human[7] abilities, and the expression of these in a particular eco-cultural niche as in so-called 'African infant motor precocity'.[8]

In order to unpack 'learning' further, consider the entries in Table 1, below: various habits, beliefs, skills, values, manners, virtues and traits have been categorised as being accountable primarily in terms of having been learned, inborn, or due to both 'nurture' and 'nature'.[9]

---

[2] Feldman, D.H. and Fowler, R.C., 'The nature(s) of developmental change: Piaget, Vygotsky, and the transition process', *New Ideas in Psychology*, 15/3 (1998), 195–210.
[3] Piaget, J., *Adaptation and Intelligence: Organic Selection and Phenocopy* (Chicago: University of Chicago Press, 1980); Piaget, J., *The Development of Thought*, trans. A. Rosin (Oxford: Basil Blackwell, 1977); and Piaget, J., *The Psychology of Intelligence* (New Jersey: Littlefield, Adams and Co., 1976).
[4] Vygotsky, L.S., *Mind in Society. The Development of Higher Psychological Processes*, Cole, M., John-Steiner, V., Scribner, S. and Souberman, E. (eds.) (Cambridge, MA: Harvard University Press, 1978).
[5] Nowadays this opposition is no longer thought correct. Thinking tends to conceive of 'nature' and 'nurture', as well as the interaction between them, as going both deeper (into the cellular environment) and further back (our genetic heritage or evolutionary history). Cf. Ridley, M., *Nature via Nurture. Genes, Experience and What Makes Us Human* (London: Harper Perennial, 2003).
[6] Cf. Holt, J., 'Measure fore measure. The strange science of Francis Galton', *The New Yorker* (24 January 2005), 84–90.
[7] Cf. Donald E. Brown's List of Human Universals, included in Pinker, S., *The Blank Slate* (London: Penguin, 2002), 435–9; and George P. Murdock's list, included in Wilson, E.O., *Consilience. The Unity of Knowledge* (London: Abacus, 1998), 162; also Wilson (*Consilience*), 164, for a discussion of the import of universals.
[8] Leiderman, P.H., Babu, B., Kagia, J., Kraener, H.C. and Leiderman, G.F., 'African infant precocity and some social influences during the first year', *Nature*, 242/5395 (1973), 247–9.
[9] Cf. Cavalli-Sforza, L.L., *Genes, People and Languages* (London: Penguin, 2001); Dawkins. R., *The Ancestor's Tale* (London: Weidenfeld and Nicolson, 2004); LeDoux, J., *Synaptic Self. How Our Brains Become Who We Are* (London: Penguin, 2002); and Ridley, *Nature via Nurture*.

Table 1: Exercise in locating the origin of new additions to the behavioural repertoire

	Learned	In-born	A bit of both
habits	Brushing teeth	Reflexes	Tool making[10]
beliefs	Hitler's rise	Object cohesion[11]	$E=mc^2$
skills	Swimming	Walking	Language[12]
values	Conservation[13]	Self-preservation	Promiscuity
manners	Port to the left[14]	____ [15]	____
virtues	____	____	Justice[16]
traits	____	Extraversion[17]	____

---

[10] Cf. Wynn, T. and Coolidge, F.L., 'The expert Neandertal mind', *Journal of Human Evolution*, 46 (2003), 467–87.

[11] Spelke, E., 'Initial knowledge: Six suggestions', *Cognition*, 50 (1994), 431–45, suggests that 'young infants appear to have systematic knowledge in four domains: physics, psychology, number, and geometry' (433); and further on, 'Comparing the knowledge that infants possess with the knowledge that they appear to lack suggests this generalisation: initial knowledge encompasses the most reliable constraints on objects, people, sets, and places that humans recognize as adults' (435).

[12] 'For the staunchest nativist, a set of genes specifically targets domain-specific modules as the end product of their epigenesis ... Under this non-developmental view, the environment simply acts as a trigger for identifying and setting (environmentally-derived) native-tongue realizations of (pre-specified) parameters of universal grammar'; Karmiloff-Smith, A., 'Development itself is the key to understanding developmental disorders', *Trends in Cognitive Science*, 2/10 (1998), 389–98.

[13] Diamond, J., *Collapse. How Societies Choose to Fail or Succeed* (New York: Viking, 2005).

[14] Passing the port to the left (or right) is such a silly, class-based affectation, that it serves as a good illustration of something, manners in this case, learned in specific circumstances by members of a group; cf. Norbert. E., *The Civilizing Process. The History of Manners and State Formation and Civilization* (Oxford: Blackwell, 1997).

[15] These could be completed in line with one's view of human nature, or a particular theory of the interaction between organism and environment; cf. Donald E. Brown's 'List of Human Universals', in Pinker, *The Blank Slate*, 435–9; and Ridley, M., *Nature via Nurture*.

[16] I chose justice because it is probably the best known virtue, and also the one most open to questions about our natural inclinations versus what must be achieved through institutions; cf. Comte-Sponville, A., *A Short Treatise on the Great Virtues. The Uses of Philosophy in Everyday Life* (London: Vintage, 2003); O'Neill, O., *Bounds of Justice* (Cambridge: CUP, 2000); and O'Neill, O., *Towards Justice and Virtue. A Constructive Account of Practical Reasoning* (Cambridge: CUP, 1996).

[17] The so-called 'Big Five' personality traits are: Extraversion, Emotional Stability, Agreeableness, Conscientiousness, and Openness to Experience; a vast literature exists on this. Cf. http://www.personalityresearch.org/ .

I am sure each reader would want to add and subtract, as well as change entries in the table above. The point of the exercise is to show that the origin or source of the new is neither obvious nor certain, i.e. not representing a perfect theory-data fit. In finding apt examples for each category, one wants to say, in each case, 'it depends' – and it usually depends on (a) one's theoretical orientation (not only as far as learning goes), (b) the particularity or generality of the new one has in mind, (c) the age/life stage of the person, and (d) the culture or context of the group exhibiting the new habit, etc. under examination.

If we should add to the list specific skills (e.g. software writing/designing), knowledge (e.g. calculus), and genius (e.g. Mozart's early ability to compose music), it becomes even more difficult to know what (and how much of it) is learned, what depends on some basic knowledge or innate competence, capacity, or talent, and what relies on a particular mixture of these.

4.1 Reflections on 'learning'

We tend to think of something as being a product of our or others' (conscious, deliberate) efforts – i.e. as having been *learned* – when: (a) we can date or place the acquisition (e.g. when, how, and where one learned to drive a car), (b) what is acquired shows greater variation than one would expect from what is inborn (e.g. individual and cultural styles of doing things, and choices about whether to do something at all[18]), and (c) behaviour shows clear changes across time and place

---

[18] We think, for example, of all people as having certain 'rites of passage' – i.e. we think of this as a human universal – but only rarely do we meet a particular content and form such as described for some Australian Aborigine societies, where 'a boy being initiated was expected to repeatedly hit his penis with a heavy rock until it was bruised and bloody. He also had several of his incisor teeth knocked out with a sharp rock by the adult men who were instructing him in the duties and obligations of manhood and the secrets of their religion'. See http://anthro.palomar.edu/social/default.htm in particular 'rites of passage'. In South Africa nowadays there is a great deal of discussion about the Zulu tradition of inspecting girls' virginity at a certain stage, and the Xhosa practice of male circumcision; the former offends defenders of human and women's rights, and the latter causes concern because of botched operations far away from medical facilities and care. My point is, we are all human indeed, and we all do very similar things, but the detail (where the proverbial Devil lives) divides us quite sharply too.

(e.g. fashions in clothing). These intuitions are however not all equally well supported by evidence. I leave this at that for now.

We also note that individuals come to know and do a great many things they were *not* clearly born with. Moreover, these skills and particular knowledge tend, more often than not, to increase in complexity and range over time until they start to fail during senescence (e.g. the daily, ordinary tasks any/all individuals learn to do from tying shoe laces to remembering important dates). In addition, the ongoing life of a specific group (or culture) attests to the fact that members of that group, including the least able, continue to learn to become like others of their kind (i.e. learn the same language, beliefs, and so forth, and the skills typical of their circumstances). That is to say, enough of the habits and so on that define a group or culture is passed on to the next generation for ongoing communication between members of that group. Learning in these terms comes across as natural, i.e. as part of our natures.

One of the most complex systems of skills and knowledge that we make our own without much apparent effort or conscious attention, and in a relatively short time, is language or our mother tongue. Perhaps we would therefore say that learning to speak involves a bit of both, that is to say, some *interaction* between what is inborn (or part of our 'nature'), and what is learned (or the result of 'nurture'). That certain of our abilities, such as communicating in our mother tongue, originate from our natures *and* require some learning, and that this can be improved through deliberate instruction, is suggested by the following: (i) the *ease* with which almost all people learn to speak, (ii) that they learn to speak the language of their *context*, and (iii) that speakers could be taught voice projection, control and various other *refinements* in the way they speak. Language learning, like a number of other basic, seemingly hard-wired or inborn abilities, suggests to some the strong hand of biology or even evolution, not only in making us able to speak, but also in equipping us with the wherewithal to tune into the speech around us so as to learn.[19]

We readily accept that there are also parts of our behavioural repertoire that are *not* learned, such as certain reflexes and other automatic responses, and that these are merely part of our natures. We accept this because we cannot place how we came to do/have these, because they are very hard (if not impossible) to resist and unlearn (e.g. eye-blink response), and are more or less the same across place and time for all normal people.

Ordinarily, too, we have a clear sense that some things we only learn under highly artificial circumstances (e.g. computer programming), or with much practice and effort (e.g. pole jumping), and that sometimes these require – in addition to long hours of practice – a great deal of talent, however one defines this (e.g. playing the violin). We believe, pre-reflectively, that talents are inborn, run in families,[20] and only rarely rear their heads unexpectedly. Common sense clarifies 'talent' in this way: when individuals learn something fast, without problems and to a degree of excellence, we tend to say, 'she is a natural' and mean that she brought something inborn and special to the learning.

The belief that some talent or a general ability of some kind underlines everything we do, learn, and come to know, also finds expression in saying of those who find things hard, 'Johnny is stupid'. We tend to explain this kind of

---

[19] Evolutionary psychology is of the view that 'phylogenesis has led to increasing pre-specification for ontogenesis, such that there are genetically-coded responses to evolutionary pressures, leading, through relatively predetermined epigenesis, to hardwired circuitry for language, theory of mind, and other specific forms of higher-level cognitive processing. In this "Swiss army knife" view of the brain, domain specificity is the starting point of ontogenesis, with development relegated to a relatively secondary role. A different view is that although evolution has pre-specified many constraints on development, it has made the human neocortex increasingly flexible and open to learning during postnatal development. In other words, evolution is argued to have selected for adapted outcomes and a strong capacity to learn, rather than prior knowledge ... [from] such a perspective, it is more plausible to think in terms of a variety of what one might call domain-relevant mechanisms that might gradually become domain-specific as a result of processing different kinds of input'; Karmiloff-Smith, 'Development', 391.

[20] I am thinking here of Francis Galton's ideas about 'nature versus nurture' and his work on 'Hereditary Genius'; cf. Holt, 'Measure fore measure', 84–90.

'slowness' by references to what is lacking (e.g. brain power, talent, motivation, and so forth), or invoke particular handicaps in the life of the person that prevent learning (e.g. 'her mother died when she was born', or 'they are very poor').

The point, however, is that the speed and efficiency with which something new is learned, and the excellence achieved in problem-solving are not equally distributed across the population.[21] This becomes more than an educational problem when intellectual differences are thought to divide groups such as men and women, Caucasians, Asians and Black-Americans, and different socio-economic classes.[22] Consider, for example, the more or less consistent finding that 'The education of the parents and the cognitive ability of the child are probably the most important determinants of educational attainment'.[23] In addition, there is strong evidence for the high heritability of intelligence, and a strong relationship between scores on 'g' loaded tests of intelligence and scholastic achievement, and scant evidence for the modifiability of intelligence. The latter does not, of course, mean that most people entering schooling will not learn; more about this in the final chapter.

Reading through the evidence for cognitive modifiability, the realisation of learning potential, or the enhancement of mental ability/intelligence, leaves one with the odd sense that nothing really works. More worryingly, it appears that those who have what it takes improve even more through education/special interventions, and those who lack what it takes lose even that with which they

---

[21] Cf. Carroll J.B., *Human Cognitive Abilities. A Survey of Factor Analytic Studies* (Cambridge: CUP, 1993); Deary, I.J., 'Individual differences in cognition: British contributions over a century', *British Journal of Psychology*, 92 (2001), 217–37; Deary, I.J. and Caryl, P.G., 'Neuroscience and human intelligence', *Trends in Neuroscience*, 20/8 (1998), 365–71; and Snow, R.E., 'Individual differences in the design of educational programs', *American Psychologists*, 41/10 (1986), 1029–39.
[22] Cf. Hernstein, R.J. and Murray, C., *The Bell Curve: Intelligence and Class Structure in American Life* (New York: The Free Press, 1994); Jensen, A.R., *The G Factor. The Science of Mental Ability* (London: Praeger, 1998); Jensen, A.R., 'Jensen on "Jensenism"', *Intelligence*, 26/3 (1998), 181–208; Jensen, A.R., *Bias in Mental Testing* (London: Methuen, 1980); and Rushton, J.P., 'The "Jensen Effect" and the "Spearman-Jensen Hypothesis" of black-white IQ differences', *Intelligence*, 26/3 (1998), 217–25.
[23] Ganzach, Y., 'Parents' education, cognitive ability, educational expectations and educational attainment: Interactive effects', *British Journal of Educational Psychology*, 70 (2000), 419–41.

90

started. We experience this as odd because we want to believe that whatever native abilities people (and many other animals too) have are plastic enough to allow for change through specialised intervention.[24] Indeed education, and various forms of therapy and politics, depend on this belief. Yet, when this intuitive sense of our plasticity or educability is subjected to rigorous empirical scrutiny, the results are more often than not disappointing or, at best, inconclusive.[25]

For those concerned with minimising the negative impact of the differences between us (e.g. group and/or individual discrepancies from intellectual or other norms), knowing how to improve on learning outcomes is therefore crucial. In this regard, the often negligible effects of concerted efforts to improve learning through special projects open up difficult debates and questions about our universal human heritage, versus how these abilities are formed and shaped (and malformed and misshaped) under specific biological, social and other conditions (e.g. *Head Start*,[26] *The Milwaukee Project*,[27] *The Abecedarian Early Intervention Project*[28]).[29] All is not lost though, if we are to take seriously the work of Reuven Feuerstein,[30] those inspired by his efforts, and those who refined some of this.[31] We return to this after introducing Vygotsky's views on learning, below.

---

[24] See Quartz, S.R., 'The constructivist brain', *Trends in Cognitive Science*, 3/2 (1999), 48, who notes: '... the evidence suggests that cortical development involves the progressive elaboration of neural circuits in which experience-dependent neural growth mechanisms act alongside intrinsic developmental processes to construct the representations underlying mature skills'. Karmiloff-Smith, 'Development', makes a similar point when showing that development is itself causal as far as the kind of mind that develops is concerned.
[25] Cf. Caroll, *Human Cognitive Abilities*.
[26] http://www.acf.hhs.gov/programs/hsb/ .
[27] http://www.uwex.edu/news/story.cfm/523 .
[28] http://www.fpg.unc.edu/~abc/ .
[29] Cf. Hernstein and Murray, *The Bell Curve*.
[30] Feuerstein, R., *The Dynamic Assessment of Retarded Performers* (Baltimore: University Park Press, 1979); and Feuerstein, R., Rand, Y., Hoffman, M.B. and Miller, R. *Instrumental Enrichment. An Intervention Program for Cognitive Modifiability* (Baltimore: University Park Press, 1980); Kozulin, A. (ed.), *The Ontogeny of Cognitive Modifiability. Applied Aspects of Mediated Learning Experience and Instrumental Enrichment. Proceedings of the International Conference* (Jerusalem: ICELP, 1997).
[31] Hamers, J.H.M., Sijtsma, K. and Riujssenaars, A.J.J.M., *Learning Potential Assessment. Theoretical, Methodological and Practical Issues* (Amsterdam: Swets and Zeitlinger, 1993); and Luther, M., Cole, E. and Gamlin, P., *Dynamic Assessment for Instruction. From Theory to Application* (York, CA: Captus University Press, 1996).

We may emphasise, at this point in our reflections on learning, that we can find ample evidence for, and examples of, learning all around us. But, we also find enough instances of problems and cases of failed instruction or lack of learning to worry about the meaning and status of the term. It is also worth reiterating that our reflection highlights a number of outstanding issues about the differences between us. We are, however, hard pressed to overcome some of these problems or to explain fully what we apparently observe or encounter in the practice of teaching. For example, we cannot say for certain in each case that it is learning, and only learning (in the sense of experiences inscribing something new in our brains, bodies, muscles, personalities, etc.) that is at work; or, alternatively, whether new additions to the repertoire only *appear* to be new but have, in fact, always been present – like the oak waiting in the acorn. And, finally, we cannot say for certain if and when as well as to what degree the new involves a bit of what we are born with, a bit of what matures in time, and a bit of what we learn in the course of particular experiences or even as a result of deliberate instruction.

We are therefore not at all clear on just how and when learning occurs (or fails to occur), which (neural, cognitive, social) mechanisms are involved, how to improve on it, and so forth. This does not, however, stop us 'telling', 'demonstrating', 'teaching',[32] and trying by all manner of means to get others to learn through deliberate instruction. Moreover, these attempts are often sufficiently successful – or at least *appear* to be so – to motivate teachers to continue. When learning does not occur, we usually look out for what *blocks* it; for example, (a) biological impairments such as sensory deficits; (b) cultural blocks such as values against girls or women learning specific skills or knowledge; (c) social blocks such as poverty and lack of access to stimulation or learning opportunities; and (d) psychological blocks such as reactions to severe trauma, lack of motivation, or low intelligence. It is obvious that while certain blocks can be attended to without much on the spot research effort (e.g. correcting

---

[32] These are placed in inverted commas to stress how uncertain their status also is – yet more names for problems.

poor eyesight), others might need careful, expert attention (e.g. treating depression due to trauma), and yet others might require considerable input from cognitive science (e.g. dealing with certain differences in the classroom). Furthermore, obtaining a clearer understanding of the constraints on learning will allow for differentiating learning that occurs more or less spontaneously, from instances or situations that require consistent input, practice and so on. Lastly, data on the limits of cognitive modifiability will facilitate fitting together more precisely teaching, task, and learning.

With regard to certain blocks to learning, I would say, *generally speaking,* that the ages and life-stages usually involved in schooling mean that teachers might as well take heart from our considerable biological, social and psychological plasticity. It is only much later on in our lives that we lose enough of this for learning and change to be thought of as problems. This is however to ignore for the moment particular cases where problems with deliberate attempts to modify specific performances are encountered, as introduced above; problems that underline both our biological capacity to change, and the contexts of lives. More about this in Chapter 5.

About teaching we may note, briefly, that each question about and perspective on learning creates quite another view on teaching. Defining 'teaching' as any deliberate attempt to create new additions to the system's repertoire, or to influence learning through instruction, means, for example, that if the new happens either spontaneously or is totally dependent on what is innate, there clearly is no role for teaching. Schooling, then, becomes at best a site holding resources, and teachers become the facilitators who remove any obstacles to learning. If learning requires something from both what is inborn and what is achieved, the question turns to what teaching should focus on and how to ensure a productive interaction between what nature supplies and schooling presents.

The image of the teacher or teaching conveyed in those very emotional and popular films such as *Goodbye Mister Chips, Dead Poets Society, To Sir With*

Love, and *Dangerous Minds* is certainly interesting in view of our reflections on learning. In these films the teacher is portrayed as someone special, someone perhaps best thought of in religious or quasi-religious terms, who will transform his disciples. These ideals or sentiments tap into a dream of teaching as some kind of transformative experience, perhaps harking back to older conceptions of education (as indeed involving the religious instruction of a small, select group). My point is that these sentimental and popular images involve models of learning that are probably not only inaccurate when we consider the process of learning modern, scientific and secular knowledge, technology, and related skills, but also anachronistic. This might just suggest another impediment to improving schooling.

It is then to *applied cognition* that I propose we turn for answers about the questions highlighted above. Further, it is in the *study of cognition* that I believe we will find a knowledge base to explore the three theses about learning suggested by our reflections:

- Learning is ubiquitous unless blocked;
- Biology (brains and bodies) directs the course of learning; and
- Context exploits and/or limits our plasticity.

We return to these three theses in the final chapter. Note, too, that it is because I believe that teachers will do better if they apply knowledge than turn to this or that specific theory, principle, or fact about learning, that I engaged in the reflections above – before casting a more formal, theoretical frame over learning, below.[33]

---

[33] Cf. http://findarticles.com/p/articles/mi_qa3671/is_200401 .

94

4.2 What we bring to learning

The one thing B.F. Skinner's behaviourism[34] gave the world is great clarity on learning, albeit at the cost of attending to more complex forms of cognition. A really amusing piece by his students is quoted in Pinker's *The Blank Slate*:

> Keller and Marian Breland reported that when they tried to use his techniques to train animals to insert poker chips into vending machines, the chickens pecked the chips, the racoons washed them, and the pigs tried to root them with their snouts.[35]

It is amusing because it shows that even these lowly creatures bring something of themselves, their *natures* or certain innate capacities, to the task of learning. The questions are: how much, and what, do we bring, and how is this structured or even released in time, through development, and in particular situations or contexts? Phrased in the terms of the topic under discussion: what is the relationship between development and learning, or how do we overcome what Pascual-Leone calls 'Plato's problem?'[36]

---

[34] Cf. Graham, G, 'Behaviorism', in Zalta, E.N. (ed.), *The Stanford Encyclopedia of Philosophy* (Fall 2002 Edition), URL =
<http://plato.stanford.edu/archives/fall2002/entries/behaviorism/> .
[35] Pinker, *The Blank Slate*, 20.
[36] Pascual-Leone clarifies this as follows: 'One of these problems is how to differentiate two irreducible modes of cognitive processing, the *conceptual* (logico-mathematical, logological, or generic knowledge – *high cognitive functions*) versus the *experiential* (perceptual-motor/spatiotemporal, infralogical, or knowledge of particulars – *low cognitive functions*); while at the same time explaining the emergence of both modes of processing from the same origin: that is, as resulting from interactions among innateness (maturation) and experience (learning, culturally mediated or direct). The other problem is that of continuous representation: How is it that perceptual or "conceptual" processual forms (codes, schemes) can in fact adapt to the evolving constraints of hard reality (the world of the senses and of learned experience) so as to embody these constraints, even in truly novel situations, where subjects lack proper representational forms'; Pascual-Leone, J., 'Vygotsky, Piaget, and the problem of Plato', *Swiss Journal of Psychology* 55/2/3 (1996), 84–92. See also Pascual-Leone, J., 'Attentional, dialectic, and mental effort: Toward an organismic theory of life-stages', in Commons, M.L., Richards, F.A. and Armon, A.C. (eds.), *Beyond Formal Operations: Late Adolescent and Adult Cognitive Development* (New York: Praeger, 1984); Pascual-Leone, J. and Baillargeon, R., 'Developmental measurement of mental attention', *International Journal of Behavioural Development*, 17/1 (1994), 161–200; and Pascual-Leone, J. and Goodman, D., *Intelligence and Experience: A Neo-Piagetian Approach. Report No. 81* (York, Ontario: York University, Department of Psychology, June 1979).

Pascual-Leone writes that it has been known since Plato that learning is impossible except against so rich a stock of prior knowledge that it reduces to recollection. Phrased in different terms:

> By quantifying this innate knowledge as inductive bias, decades of work in formal learning theory reinforced this paradox: learning is too hard without first severely restructuring what can be learned. Unconstrained, or *tabula rasa*, learning is infeasible. This suggests that the major hurdle in acquiring cognitive skills is not one involving statistical inference *per se*. Rather, it is the prior issue of the source of appropriate representations that make learning possible at all.[37]

Then, too, the question of the emergence of new representations, or how greater complexity can emerge from simple beginnings, is an old battleground between theorists,[38] as noted in the previous chapter. Here I want to underline a kind of consensus about learning: *it takes a whole lot from nature to get the new going.*[39]

On the view that 'all our knowledge is derived from our experience',[40] *learning* takes the lion's share of what it takes to – what does one say? – become human, express our species-being, acquire the knowledge and skills appropriate for a particular place and time, attain individual excellence, and know *what* to do, *where* and *when*. Is learning merely another label for that process by which the assumed 'white paper' or *tabula rasa* is written on?[41]

Educationally speaking, an empiricist view of knowledge casts a positive light on the importance of learning, and on the irreplaceable role of the teacher in this process. Very few post-'60s educators would, however, admit to *being* an

---

[37] Cf. Quartz, 'The constructivist brain', 48–57.
[38] Cf. Fodor, J.A., *A Theory of Content and Other Essays* (Cambridge, MA: MIT Press, 2002); Fodor, J.A., *Psychosemantics* (Cambridge, MA: MIT Press, 1987); Fodor, J.A., *Representations* (Cambridge, MA: MIT Press, 1981), 257–316; and Bickhard, M.H., 'Commentary: On the cognition in cognitive development', *Developmental Review*, 19 (1999), 369–88.
[39] Cf. Ridley, *Nature via Nurture*.
[40] A 'central tenet of empiricism', according to Dancy. J., *Introduction to Contemporary Epistemology* (Oxford: Basil Blackwell, 1989), 53.
[41] Pinker, *The Blank Slate*, 5, quotes the relevant bit from John Locke as follows: 'Let us then suppose the mind to be, as we say, white paper void of all characters, without any ideas. How comes it to be furnished? Whence comes it by that vast store which the busy and boundless fancy of man has painted on it with an almost endless variety? Whence has it all the materials of reason and knowledge? To this I answer, in one word, from EXPERIENCE'.

empiricist, because of some convoluted set of commitments that has turned this into an unwelcome tag.

The taint of empiricism has to do with a certain positive evaluation of the social and cultural aspects of knowledge-making, in contrast to what Shapin calls 'individualistic empiricism',[42] or the 17th century's 'rejection of trust and authority in the pursuit of natural knowledge'.[43] So that some of the ingredients going into this (cognitively, emotionally, politically, and morally) *mixed* assessment of empiricism as a theory of knowledge have to do with a rejection of Enlightenment ambitions, and with lauding a more relativistic and humanistic temper,[44] rather than with a commitment to another view of knowledge.

Reasonableness demands, however, that empiricism be assessed on the basis of its adequacy as an explanation of its object, i.e. whether and to what degree it answers (or fails to answer) criticism of its tenets, and its fit with the data on the object of the theory (knowledge, in this case). Empiricism is thought to fail because we know more than experience could have furnished us with (cf. Chomsky's debate with Skinner about 'verbal learning' or the adequacy of the S-R explanation for the acquisition of a mother tongue).[45] In contrast to empiricism, we may opt for rationalism[46] as an overall epistemological frame for answering the question about what we bring to learning.

---

[42] Shapin, S., *The Scientific Revolution* (Chicago: University of Chicago Press, 1996), 72.

[43] *Idem.*

[44] Cf. Toulmin, S., *Cosmopolis. The Hidden Agenda of Modernity* (New York: The Free Press, 1990).

[45] Chomsky, N., 'Review of Skinner's *Verbal Behavior*', *Language*, 35 (1959), 26–58; and Skinner, B.F., *Verbal Behavior* (New York: Appleton-Century-Crofts, 1957).

[46] According to Markie, to be a rationalist is to adopt at least one of three claims:

1. The Intuition/Deduction Thesis: Some propositions in a particular subject area, S, are knowable by us by intuition alone; still others are knowable by being deduced from intuited propositions. (Intuition and deduction thus provide us with knowledge *a priori*, which is to say knowledge gained independently of sense experience.)

2. The Innate Knowledge Thesis: We have knowledge of some truths in a particular subject area, S, as part of our rational nature. (Our innate knowledge is not learned through either sense experience or intuition and deduction. It is just part of our nature. Experiences may trigger a process by which we bring this knowledge to consciousness, but the experiences do not provide us with the knowledge itself. It has in some way been with us all along.)

The opposition between empiricism and rationalism is the very focus of Piaget's 'constructivist epistemology', which not only involves both knowledge through experience (acting on objects), and what the mind imposes on that experience, but also internal re-organisation towards more complex forms of action and knowledge.[47] Piaget's constructivism[48] is aimed at explaining the origin and growth of knowledge from sensory-motor action to logical-mathematical structures through the process of equilibration. Central to the concept of equilibration are the regulatory mechanisms of 'assimilation' (i.e. the incorporation of objects into cognitive structures),[49] and 'accommodation' (i.e. when the particularities of an object create cognitive disequilibrium). Piaget writes, of equilibration:

... we do not mean we can identify a single general structure of equilibrium which can be stated once and for all, and applied to every situation and to every level ... but rather we can observe a process (hence the term 'equilibration') leading from certain states of equilibrium to others, qualitatively different, and passing through multiple 'non-balances' and equilibriums.[50]

Piaget describes three forms of equilibration as follows: the first has to do with 'the fundamental interaction of the (epistemic) subject and the objects (or

3. The Innate Concept Thesis: We have some of the concepts we employ in a particular subject area, S, as part of our rational nature. (They are part of our rational nature in such a way that, while sense experiences may trigger a process by which they are brought to consciousness, experience does not provide the concepts or determine the information they contain.) Note the distinctions between *propositions* (e.g. "It rained last night"), *truths* (e.g. mathematical theorems), and *concepts* (e.g. a label for an abstract category); Markie, P., 'Rationalism vs. Empiricism', in Zalta, E.N. (ed.), *The Stanford Encyclopedia of Philosophy* (Fall 2004 Edition), URL = <http://plato.stanford.edu/archives/fall2004/entries/rationalism-empiricism/>.
[47] Cf. Fabricius, W.V., 'Piaget's theory of knowledge. Its philosophical context', *Human Development*, 26 (1983), 325–34.
[48] Note that 'Constructivism is the Piagetian notion that learning leads the child to develop new types of representations'; Marcus, G.F., 'Can connectionism save constructivism?', *Cognition*, 66/2 (1998), 153–82.
[49] 'I incorporate the object into my cognitive structures because I *act toward it in a certain way*, just as the child who sucks a thumb is assimilating it to a sucking scheme. I engage in an act of judging, interpreting, or bringing the object under a certain (cognitive) category. Hence, *assimilation is the equivalent of a judgement*: to assimilate a thumb is to judge the thumb as something to be sucked'; Kitchener, R.F., *Piaget's* Theory of Knowledge. *Genetic Epistemology and Scientific Reason* (New Haven: Yale University Press, 1986), 53.
[50] Piaget, *The Development of Thought*, 3.

98

world/reality). This involves an equilibration between the assimilation of schemes of action and the accommodation of these to the objects'.[51] This first form of equilibration is what sets the development of knowledge in motion. The second form of equilibration revolves around the interactions between the subsystems or the various schemes and structures that result from the first form of equilibration. Piaget said that the various subsystems are generally constructed at different speeds, a situation that causes various non-balances in the cognitive system and requires resolution or a higher form of equilibrium. The third form of equilibration involves the establishment of a hierarchy of schemes and structures. This involves an ordering of subsystems in relation to the totality that includes them.

The different kinds of equilibration refer, therefore, to three modes of development, from the most basic, which occurs when the subject acts on the objects in the environment; to the next mode, which emphasises the interactions between the knowledge gained from/constructed through the actions performed on objects; to the last mode, which indicates the formation of a totality of knowledge about the world, and where the different schemes are integrated, co-ordinated, and ordered in relation to one another and the whole. Piaget's comments on non-balances in the cognitive system are worth including:

> It is worthwhile to note that however the non-balance arises it produces the driving force of development. Without this, knowledge remains static. But non-balance also plays a release role, since its fecundity is measured by the possibility of surmounting it, in other words, of reaching a higher form of equilibrium. It is therefore evident that the real source of progress is to be sought in both the insufficiency responsible for the conflict and the improvement expressed in the equilibrium.[52]

I leave Piaget's ideas about the origin and growth of knowledge with this very short overview of equilibration. Of note is the degree to which his focus is on mechanisms and processes *internal* to the cognitive system.

---

[51] *Ibid.*, 9.
[52] *Ibid.*, 13.

We return below to the move away from modelling ever increasing complexity 'internally', to explaining greater sophistication in problem-solving by situating the body and brain in a world rich with possibilities for extending these innate capabilities.[53] The move away from the internal, mental theatre – a move that characterises recent theorising about cognition – is to a considerable extent motivated by specific empirical challenges to classical cognitivism. Elizabeth Spelke, for instance, challenges

> ... the traditional view that psychological and neural development proceed from peripheral to central structures, such that humans first sense things and respond to them reflexively, later perceive things and act on them adaptively, and finally begin to think about things that leave their view.[54]

This is interesting because her empirical work suggests that there is a core of *initial* knowledge that furnishes the basic constraints on the objects, people, sets, and places that humans recognise as adults. Moreover, such initial knowledge is, according to Spelke, innate, domain-specific, and task specific,[55] which neatly gets us to the next epistemological position that I want to introduce. Before this, note that such initial knowledge could be regarded as overcoming the learning problem, or Plato's problem, introduced above.

'Evolutionary epistemology' is about various attempts to address questions of knowledge by providing an evolutionary account of the development of cognitive structures, and analysing the development of human knowledge and epistemological norms by appealing to relevant biological considerations.[56] The mechanisms involved in knowledge (e.g. brains, sensory systems, and motor systems) are obvious concerns in the study of cognition, as we saw in the previous chapter. Moreover, evolutionary epistemology is a naturalised approach to

---

[53] Cf. Hutchins, E., *Cognition in the Wild* (Cambridge, MA: The MIT Press, 1995).

[54] Spelke, E., 'Initial knowledge: Six suggestions', *Cognition*, 50 (1994), 431–45.

[55] Cf. http://cogweb.ucla.edu/CogSci/Spelke.html .

[56] See Horvath, C.D., 'Interactionism and innateness in the evolutionary study of human nature', *Biology and Philosophy*, 15 (2000), 321–37; this is well worth reading for its clarification of central notions discussed in evolutionary psychology, and various positions on the relationship between 'nature' and 'nurture', viz., biological determinists, social constructionists, interactionists, and those supporting developmental systems theory.

100

questions about knowledge, and thus relies on empirical results of particular sciences such as biology and psychology to resolve issues arising in questions about knowledge and conceptual change.[57] A central tenet of evolutionary epistemology is that as natural beings, with a particular evolutionary history, people's

> ... capacities for knowledge and belief are also the products of a natural evolutionary development. As such, there is some reason to suspect that knowing, as a natural activity, could and should be treated and analysed along lines compatible with its status, i.e., by the methods of natural science.[58]

An evolutionary approach to knowledge is to be seen in the work of Millikan[59] and of Pinker.[60] Millikan, for example, emphasises selection for proper functions,[61] or the specific brain mechanisms/modules underlying certain abilities (e.g. language),[62] in a manner that emphasises both the selection *for* certain functions, and the fact that these function like bodily organs. Pinker's work brings together the notion of adaptation and mental computation (dubbed an example of 'New Synthesis' theories by Fodor, as we saw in Chapter 3). As Fodor puts it,

---

[57] Bradie, M., and Harms, W., 'Evolutionary Epistemology', in Zalta, E.N. (ed.), *The Stanford Encyclopedia of Philosophy* (Spring 2004 Edition), URL = <http://plato.stanford.edu/archives/spr2004/entries/epistemology-evolutionary/> .
[58] *Idem.*
[59] Millikan, R.G., *White Queen Psychology and Other Essays for Alice* (Cambridge, MA: The MIT Press, 1995); and Millikan, R.G., *Language, Thought, and Other Biological Categories* (Cambridge, MA: The MIT Press, 1984).
[60] Pinker, S., *How the Mind Works* (London: Penguin, 1997); and Pinker, *The Blank Slate*.
[61] Millikan, *White Queen Psychology*, emphasises the history of something (rather than its present properties or dispositions) to talk about its proper function. She writes, 'Easy cases of items having proper functions are body organs and instinctive behaviours. A proper function of such an organ or behaviour is, roughly, a function that its ancestors have performed that has helped account for proliferation of the genes responsible for it, hence helped account for its own existence. But the definition of "proper function" covers, univocally, the functions of many other items as well, including the functions of learned behaviours, reasoned behaviours, customs, language devices such as words and syntactic forms, and artifacts' (14). Also relevant for our purposes here is her argument, 'that [the] normal perceptual and cognitive function for contemporary humans is a *proper* function of their brains' (46).
[62] Cf. Cummins, D.D. and Cummins, R., 'Biological preparedness and evolutionary explanation', *Cognition*, 73/3 (1999), 37–53, for a non-modular and non-innate view on evolutionary explanations.

'What's new about the New Synthesis is mostly the consequence of conjoining a rationalist epistemology with a syntactic notion of mental computation.'[63]

The view that the brain and mind or cognition (and what they do, and how they do so) are pre-specified, or that these have been shaped by evolution for specific tasks, is popular among those who abide by an evolutionary epistemology, but is nonetheless still contentious.[64] For example, evolutionary psychologists like Cosmides and Tooby explain our competencies for specific tasks in terms of what has evolved; and, given the time-frame for change imposed by evolution, they explain what we can (or cannot) do in terms of what was typical of our hunter-gatherer past.[65] This is, however, most unsatisfying because it renders opaque the new. It cannot explain our ability – albeit not that widespread – to perform in logically optimal, deductively valid, and creative (or truly novel) ways on abstract and unfamiliar tasks. But, that 'we' in fact do so underlies all innovation, discoveries and change.

The point of this brief overview of three prominent views on the origin of knowledge is to underline different backgrounds to ideas about what we bring to learning. As noted, from an *empiricist* point of view, learning (or experience) is what it takes to display the new. *Rationalism*, in turn, emphasises the shape of what we are or have *a priori*; and an *evolutionary epistemology* puts the burden on evolved modules set for particular encounters. In an interesting sense, rationalism and evolutionary epistemology both outline what is there in (or as part of) us

[63] Fodor, *The Mind Doesn't Work That Way*, 12.
[64] Cf. Fodor, *The Mind Doesn't Work That Way*; and Lloyd, E., 'Evolutionary psychology: The burdens of proof', *Biology and Philosophy*, 14 (1999), 211–33.
[65] Central to assessing what is 'natural' to assume about people and what they are good for/good at, comes from the kind of thinking illustrated in the following: '… our ancestors spent the last two million years before that as one kind of forager or another. These relative spans are important because they establish which set of environments and conditions defined the adaptive problems the mind was shaped to cope with: Pleistocene conditions, rather than modern conditions. This conclusion stems from the fact that the evolution of complex design is a slow process when contrasted with historical time'; Barkow, J.H., Cosmides, L. and Tooby, J., *The Adapted Mind. Evolutionary Psychology and the Generation of Culture* (Oxford: OUP, 1992), 5. That this evolution might not be all that slow is argued by Bloom, H., 'Instant evolution. The influence of the city on human genes: A speculative case', *New Ideas in Psychology*, 19/3 (2001), 203–20.

before learning. This is perhaps one reason why the nativism of Chomsky is often claimed by thinkers of a different stripe to him.[66]

These three positions also cast a different light on the problem of change, or adaptation to new and unfamiliar tasks or situations. For example, if learning alone must inscribe the blank slate, learning the new or making the unfamiliar our own is a mystery (as noted above regarding 'Plato's problem'). If what is innate suffices to bring about the new, then a great deal of variation in competencies across time and place and (individual as well as cultural) difference in the expression of these are strange. And if evolution has to do with what it takes to learn, know and act in familiar and novel – as well as truly novel – ways, then it is a mystery that we are not still hunting and gathering – or that we got to that stage at all!

4.3 Intelligence and unfamiliar territory

Plotkin writes:

> *The evolution of intelligence switches the focus of causation to those behaviours that are driven by intelligence from genes and development to the processes and mechanisms of intelligence.* The logic of the analysis of evolved intelligence tells us that the behaviour of intelligent animals cannot be understood purely in terms of genes – if it could it would be a contradiction, because then intelligence would not have evolved.[67]

What is particularly interesting about this for my purposes is the idea that intelligence itself is a productive force, that is to say, it creates the products that enable and transform action. As such, it is this natural ability that allows us to reach into unfamiliar territory. It is also worth pointing out, however, that the products of intelligence – for example, particular cultural habits, practices, and so on – will facilitate certain, but not all, reaches into unfamiliar territory. This is an issue of particular concern for coping with differences in the classroom.

---

[66] See Fodor's discussion of differences between Chomsky's nativism and the rest (*The Mind Doesn't Work That Way*, 8–22).

[67] Plotkin, H., *The Imagined World Made Real* (London: Penguin, 2003), 74; author's emphasis.

In *The Imagined World Made Real*, Plotkin focuses specifically on culture as probably the most remarkable product of our evolved intelligence, one that makes us appear quite different from other animals, with whom we nonetheless share a great deal of biology. Yet 'culture' is certainly also the source of a great deal of conflict and a great many difficulties in multicultural societies, as has been pointed out throughout this volume.

The pre-eminent theorist of culture and cognition is of course Vygotsky, whose work (as noted in previous chapters) is experiencing a kind of rebirth thanks to distributed or situated views of cognition. Vygotsky considered the Stimulus-Response (S-R) framework unsuitable for the study of higher psychological processes. His main objection to this involved his views on the importance of sign and tool use. He wrote:

> One thing is already certain. Just as the first use of tools refutes the notion that development represents the mere unfolding of the child's organically predetermined system of activity, so the first use of signs demonstrates that there cannot be a single organically predetermined internal system of activity that exists for each psychological function. The use of artificial means, the transition to mediated activity, fundamentally, changes all psychological operations just as the use of tools limitlessly broadens the range of activities within which the new psychological functions may operate. In this context, we can use the term higher psychological function, or higher behaviour as referring to the combination of tool and sign in psychological activity.[68]

In the above quotation, it is crucial to note that Vygotsky makes two rather deadly strikes. His first is against those who favour one or the other purely evolutionary view on what we bring to situations and also to aspects of Piaget's view on development (i.e. in what he has to say against 'the mere unfolding of the child's organically predetermined system of activity', and the view that there is 'a single organically predetermined internal system of activity that exists for each psychological function').[69] Vygotsky's second strike is against simplistic views on

---

[68] Vygotsky, *Mind in Society*, 55.
[69] It is well enough known that Piaget proposed a stage-like development of increasingly more complex and better-integrated, logical structures. Case clarifies this as follows: 'a "logical

context or, then, stimuli emitted by the environment (the S-R framework). Central to both of these is Vygotsky's idea that *tools* and *signs* transform both context and activity. In these terms, it is clear how different Vygotsky's ideas are from those of theorists who emphasise context, but in some uni-dimensional/-directional way (i.e. behaviourists), and how much closer his ideas are to the views of Clark and others introduced above (and to which we turn again in the final chapter).

In order to access and explain higher forms of behaviour, Vygotsky advocated what he called an 'experimental-developmental' method, one that 'artificially provokes or creates a process of psychological development'.[70] This means that tasks must be set that will *elicit change*, or *provoke cognitive adaptation*. The aim of Vygotsky's proposals for psychological analyses can be summarised as follows: (a) process analysis as opposed to object analysis; (b) analysis that reveals real, causal or dynamic relations as opposed to enumeration of a process's outer features, that is, explanatory, not descriptive, analysis; and (c) developmental analysis that returns to the source and reconstructs all the points in the development of a given structure.[71] These proposals for what a dynamic, explanatory analysis entails, frame (at best) what has come to be known as 'dynamic testing';[72] more about this in Chapter 5.

Vygotsky's view of learning and mind specifically underlines the importance of language, tool and sign use and the internalisation of social communication; a process through which the cultural guide (mother, caregiver, or

structure" [is] a coherent set of logical operations that can be applied to any domain of human activity and to which any cognitive task in the domain must ultimately be assimilated'. He goes on to write that 'Piaget hypothesized that the form of children's operational structures is different at different stages of their development and that this gives their thought at each stage a unique character'; Case, R., *The Mind's Staircase. Exploring the Conceptual Underpinnings of Children's Thought and Knowledge* (Hillsdale, NJ: Lawrence Erlbaum Associates, Inc., 1992), 5. Moreover, it is this view on emergence that Fodor has repeatedly criticised, as already noted. Cf. Bickhard, 'Commentary'; and Bickhard, M.H., 'The import of Fodor's anti-constructivist argument', in Steffe, L. (ed.), *Epistemological Foundations of Mathematical Experience* (New York: Springer-Verlag, 1991), 14–25.
[70] Vygotsky, *Mind in Society*, 61.
[71] *Ibid.*, 65.
[72] Cf. Grigorenko, E.L. and Sternberg, R.J., 'Dynamic testing', *Psychological Bulletin*, 124/1 (1998), 75–111, for a brief review of this.

older sibling) ensures that what occurs, at first *between* people, on the *inter*-psychological plain, becomes available for *intra*-psychological functioning. Vygotsky thought that the Zone of Proximal Development (ZPD)

> ... defines those functions that have not yet matured but are in the process of maturation, functions that will mature tomorrow but are currently in an embryonic state. These functions could be termed the 'buds' or 'flowers' of development rather that the 'fruits' of development.[73]

In these terms, therefore, the ZPD refers to

> ... the distance between the actual developmental level as determined by independent problem solving and the level of potential development as determined through problem solving under adult guidance or in collaboration with more capable peers.[74]

Of primary importance in reading the ZPD for our own purposes is Vygotsky's emphasis on the social (or cultural) nature of learning. Vygotsky and his followers tell us that each learner grows into the intellectual life around him/her; and that *what we do today with assistance we do tomorrow on our own.* This is at one and the same time a psychological theory of enculturation and learning, and a most distressing view for those whose surrounding intellectual life is itself poor or impoverished. We take on the issue of differences in the classroom specifically in the final chapter.

The relationship between cognitive operations and culture achieves a special kind of clinical or remedial focus in Feuerstein's work.[75] His ideas about 'mediated learning experiences' (MLE) are particularly noteworthy:

> By mediated learning experience (MLE) we refer to the way in which a 'mediating' agent transforms stimuli emitted by the environment, usually a

---

[73] Vygotsky, *Mind in Society*, 84.

[74] This is the formulation that is so often cited in the various attempts to determine the 'true potential' of those who do not perform as expected for their age on conventional (edumetric or psychometric) tests of the 'one-shot' kind; cf. Grigorenko and Sternberg, 'Dynamic testing', 77. I return to Vygotsky's proposal regarding dynamic, explanatory analysis and his socio-cultural theory about the origin of higher psychological functions (*Mind in Society*, 84) as a framework for assessment in the final chapter.

[75] Feuerstein, *The Dynamic Assessment of Retarded Performers*; Feuerstein, Rand, Hoffman and Miller, *Instrumental Enrichment*.

parent, sibling, or other caregiver. This mediating agent, guided by his intentions, culture, and emotional investment, selects and organises the world of stimuli for the child. The mediator selects stimuli that are most appropriate and then frames, filters, and schedules them; he determines the appearance or disappearance of certain stimuli and ignores others.[76]

In the quotation above, Feuerstein, in effect, elaborates Vygotsky's ZPD; Feuerstein emphasises the teaching (or mediating) task by stating that the mediator 'selects stimuli that are most appropriate and then frames, filters, and schedules them; he determines the appearance or disappearance of certain stimuli and ignores others'. He also thought that the more and earlier an organism is subjected to MLE, the greater would be its capacity to 'efficiently use and be affected by direct exposure to stimuli'.[77] Feuerstein regarded 'deficient cognitive functions' (which he described at the input, elaboration and output phases of cognition), as the product of a lack of, or insufficient, MLE; the latter, according to him, arise from situations where parents (or caregivers) – for one or another reason – *stop* mediating to their children (or 'deprive'[78] their children of their own culture).[79]

The biggest block to learning, in Feuersteinian terms, is therefore a lack of, or insufficient, MLE. Furthermore, his views on deficient cognitive functions resulting from a lack of, or insufficient, MLE alert us to the possibility that adaptation to western-type schooling and learning, generally, will be difficult for non-western learners (and presumably *vice versa*), because they might have to *unlearn* a great deal before they can learn the skills and knowledge typical of their adopted culture/country. As far as unlearning goes, it is important to note that the skills and insights learners obtain from everyday tasks might very well be

---

[76] Feuerstein, Rand, Hoffman and Miller, *Instrumental Enrichment*, 15.

[77] *Ibid.*, 16.

[78] For Feuerstein this was often the case when parents (or caregivers) felt insecure about the appropriateness of their skills and knowledge for their children's lives in a new cultural environment with a new, and often foreign to the parents, language.

[79] Feuerstein, Rand, Hoffman and Miller, *Instrumental Enrichment*, 71.

107

antagonistic to the discipline involved in formal, school knowledge and learning.[80] Feuerstein's own work with immigrant children in Israel culminated in the Learning Potential Assessment Device (LPAD), which inspired a great deal of work on the assessment of potential, rather than of children's manifest abilities or that which has already matured.[81]

I tested Feuerstein's elaboration of the ZPD – his specification of deficient cognitive functions in the absence of sufficient and good quality MLE – in research on mother-child interaction, and came up with what I called 'mediational operators', i.e. ideal adult mediational strategies that will produce efficient autonomous problem-solving skills in the child.[82] These, furthermore, became a basis for ongoing assessment in the work with university students.[83] My point is that there is merit in Feuerstein's clinical elaboration of Vygotsky's ZPD, in that it indicates a fruitful set of principles for application; but, as said before, this requires ongoing empirical scrutiny in particular situations. On a more theoretical level, Vygotsky's and Feuerstein's work, as well as the work of others in this tradition,[84] certainly underlines the manner in which *brains* and *bodies* become *minds* and *people* during enculturation.

---

[80] Cf. Luria, A.R., *Cognitive Development: Its Cultural and Social Foundations* (Cambridge, MA: Harvard University Press, 1976); and Vygotsky, *Mind in Society*.

[81] Cf. Grigorenko and Sternberg, 'Dynamic testing', 75–111; Hamers, Sijtsma and Riujssenaars, *Learning Potential Assessment*; and Resing, W.C.M. and van Wijk, A.M., 'Leerpotentieel: Onderzoek bij allochtone leerlingen uit het basisonderwijs', *Tijdschrift voor Orthopedagogiek*, 35 (1996), 432–44.

[82] Craig, A.P., *Mothers and Children: An Analysis of Change* (Doctoral dissertation, Department of Psychology, University of Natal, Durban, 1985), 207–68. Briefly, these mediational operators are: task readiness, gathering information, specifying means and goals, making the problem explicit, attending to detail, visual transport, emphasising invariant aspects of the task, dealing with different sources of information, discovering causal relationships, and co-ordination and integration. Note that from a distributed view of cognition, i.e. if wanting to focus learning and teaching on enhancing and extending brain and/or mind's functions, these are highly suitable for managing structuring classroom activities.

[83] Craig, A.P., 'Excellence in and through education', *South African Journal of Higher Education*, 2/1 (1988), 3–8.

[84] Cf. Cole, M. and Scribner, S., *Culture and Thought. A Psychological Introduction* (New York: John Wiley and Sons, Inc., 1974); Cole, M., *Cultural Psychology: A Once and Future Discipline* (Cambridge, MA: Harvard University Press, 1996); Cole, M., Valsiner, J., Engelström, Y., Branco, A.U. and Vasquez, O., *Mind, Culture and Activity. Seminal Papers from the Laboratory of*

108

Given an emphasis on the relationship between mind and culture, we must therefore acknowledge that the 'world' for humans is crucially different from 'the proper context' for the fish[85] in that we make, and have always made, many different, not always well-chosen, places our homes (as 'recorded' by fossil remains, and various other remains and inscriptions all the way to the act of writing history). In addition, our homes have often enough changed both by choice and through force.[86]

The most outstanding feature of our evolved intelligence is that it is this very gift that makes us *different*, and then fails us in dealing wisely and well with the very differences we increasingly have come to value, or at least *say* that we value. But rather than focus this time on the litany of problems associated with our natures (e.g. aggression, war, rape, competitiveness, and the exploitation of others), I want to highlight our *evolved ability to change*; one that allows us into territories evolution cannot and could not foresee.

Our ability to change is, of course, another way of capturing our ability to learn and, at best, to act purposively, wisely and well on what we have learned. Change is part of our *natures*: we change what we find around us,[87] are changed by what is around, and are different across situations, or time and place. How plastic we are is of more than theoretical interest to thinkers like Andy Clark, who regards our bodiliness as a negotiable boundary,[88] or Daniel Dennett, who sees the

Comparative Human Cognition (Cambridge: CUP, 1998); Valsiner, J., *The Guided Mind. A Sosiogenetic Approach to Personality* (Cambridge, MA: Harvard University Press, 1998); and Wertsch, J., *Culture, Communication and Cognition* (Cambridge, CUP, 1985).
[85] Clark, A., 'Where brain, body, and world collide', *Cognitive Systems Research*, 1/1 (1999). He writes in this that 'the real swimming machine, I suggest, is thus the fish in its proper context: the fish plus the surrounding structures and vortices that it actively creates and then maximally exploits. The cognitive machine, in the human case, looks similarly extended ...' (10).
[86] Cf. Dawkins, *The Ancestor's Tale*.
[87] Cf. Kirsh, D., 'Adapting the environment instead of oneself', *Adaptive Behavior*, 4/3/4 (1996), 415–52.
[88] Clark, A., *Natural-born Cyborgs. Minds, Technologies, and the Future of Human Intelligence* (Oxford: OUP, 2003).

self as similarly negotiable, as open to change, augmentation, and extension;[89] indeed, it is a question for everybody who wants to or must intervene in others' lives. William James, that very wise observer of people, already noted at the end of the 19th century that 'a man's Self is the sum total of all that he CAN call his own' – and he included in the list of what he can call his own, 'his clothes and his house, his wife and children, his ancestors and friends, his reputation and works, his lands and horses, and yacht and bank account ...' and he noted too that as these prosper, he feels good, and if they dwindle, he suffers.[90]

It is in these terms that I want to promote a view that the world's knowledge, technology, and skills belong to anyone and everyone – they are there for the taking, for all those able to do so. Moreover, our natural ability to change is best thought of as a resource for education to *exploit*, so that education is at best aimed at providing each self with the opportunities and wherewithal to make as much of all the world's knowledge, technology, and skills her own, or part of herself as possible. My point is that education is possible to the degree that it, as an enterprise, harnesses our adaptive capacities (to change and learn), and successful to the degree that it extends the boundaries of our selves by extending what we CAN do, know and call our own.

---

[89] Dennett, D.C., *Freedom Evolves* (London: Penguin, 2004); Dennett, D.C., *Kinds of Minds* (London: Weidenfeld and Nicolson, 1996); Dennett, D.C., *Darwin's Dangerous Idea. Evolution and the Meanings of Life* (London: Penguin, 1995); and Dennett, D.C., *Consciousness Explained* (London: Penguin, 1991).
[90] William James, quoted in LeDoux, *Synaptic Self*, 13.

CHAPTER 5

Differences in the Classroom

In this chapter I examine the differences between us from various perspectives. I consider tests of differences, and the role of culture, and I underline our ability to change. Moreover, we return to the three theses about learning suggested in Chapter 4: viz. that learning is ubiquitous unless blocked; that biology directs the course of learning; and that context exploits and/or limits our plasticity. I end the book with thoughts regarding the contexts of lives and how these influence what can be achieved.

The central business in the classroom is *learning*,[1] and of course teaching.[2] This already points to the study of cognition as the appropriate knowledge base for the enterprise of education. When, in addition to this, we come to acknowledge the multicultural contexts in which we typically engage nowadays, this domain offers even more to education, as I intend to show in what follows.

In a world without differences and one where each person learned as easily and well as the next, schooling could have proceeded without so much as a

---

[1] Cf. http://findarticles.com/p/articles/mi_qa3671/is_200401 for an overview of the state of things as far as knowing about learning goes – from the perspective of education.

[2] Cf. Demetriou, A., 'NOOPLASIS: 10 + 1 postulates about the formation of the mind', Special issue of *Learning and Instruction: The Journal of the European Association for Research in Learning and Instruction*, 8/4 (1998), for interesting ideas about teaching vis-à-vis mind or cognitive operations.

backward glance at the study of cognition. Teachers could then have got on with their subject-specific expertise as timed and scheduled by curriculum designers (who would only have needed to keep the subject-goals in mind, divided by the years of schooling).[3] This, more or less, captures the heart of highly selected or exclusive forms of education – no wonder it is an attractive model – but it is hardly, as such, a good model for mass education. Elite education chooses the groups involved, the goals and means of education, and matches the curriculum, teachers, and site for schooling so closely that differences are kept to an absolute minimum.[4]

I have argued that a focus on universally standardised skills, technology and knowledge is the proper focus of mass schooling; thus, I too advocate a kind of homogenisation, but my reasons for this are quite different from those informing the elite model. My reasons have to do with what is *possible* given limited resources and the nature of open classrooms and what is *desirable* given the nature of global exchanges. I thus want to keep personal, cultural and other group-specific identifications, commitments, values, beliefs, and projects outside the open classroom for the sake of excellence in education – excellence defined in

[3] The following in this regard is worth noting (perhaps again and again): 'The point I want to draw out from the history of the concept of "education" is that we enter schools, more or less willingly, to be schooled, trained, and instructed in that which we do *not* already understand or know, but which is thought to be necessary for our life's work. How to get a handle on someone's "life's work", and what this demands from her/his schooling, is not however at all that clear though. As we are inclined to say, the future is in principle unknowable; if we knew "it", it would no longer be in the "future". This poses very particular problems for those involved in curriculum planning. One thing that is, however, part and parcel of our future-directedness is the problem of making the as yet-unknown, known, i.e. part of one's habitual repertoire of thought and habit. Yet rarely if ever do educators *per se* raise the question about the possibility of, and limits on, understanding. I think what we take education to be, and how this contributes to our decisions regarding what kind of people to become and lives to lead are impoverished by way of this omission'; Craig, A.P., 'Education and the question about understanding', *South African Journal of Higher Education*, 15/1 (2001), 26. In this, I use three stories from Umberto Eco's *Kant and the Platypus* (London: Secker and Warburg, 1999) to examine the consequences of confronting the new or unfamiliar: (1) Marco Polo (13th century) who, on his voyages around the world, found creatures in Java that he thought of as *a new kind of unicorn*; (2) the Aztecs' first encounter with the conquistadors (16th century) and their large animals, which they had never seen before, but described as *deer as high as the roofs of the houses*; and (3) an animal, until then unknown by scientists, found in Australia on the shores of a lake – what we now recognise as the *platypus* (25–31).
[4] Cf. http://www.questia.com/search/cultural-history-education ; and http://www.questia.com/PM.qst?a=o&d=54447684 .

terms of how well schooling equips learners with control over the code. This is not without problems though; and hence the need to attend to the differences between us.

5.1 Individual differences

It does not take a great deal of skill or knowledge to note differences between people, but when it comes to handling them productively in the classroom, common sense fails us. I discussed more and less helpful approaches to this in Chapters 1 and 2.

In this section I want to examine various kinds of *tests* for assessing differences. The point is to show how this integral part of modern schooling (and society) – testing – fits into the study of cognition and facilitates (or not) handling differences.

The aim of testing is to *describe, explain* and *predict* human behaviour from one to another test or situation, and, on the basis of the norms for a group, to thus *describe, explain* and *predict* an individual's ability, inclination or behaviour in a comparable (future) situation. Phrased differently, we test because we want to know how an individual's test performance compares to others like herself; why an individual behaves as she does; and how an individual will behave and perform in future. We assume that test performance, if 'true', describes an individual's abilities, interests, or personality (depending on the specific test in question) and, as such, provides the basis from which to explain and predict future behaviour. The individual's score on a test tells us where that individual is placed against a norm group – others like herself in terms of age, sex, and so on – regarding her abilities, interests, or personality. In this way an individual's score on some or other set of measures indicates the standing, as it were, of her abilities, interests, or personality traits in relation to others of her kind.

Lubinski's[5] review of the scientific and social significance of assessing individual differences, captures the aim of testing and, as such, differential psychology, as follows:

> Differential psychology comprises the psychometric assessment of abilities, personality, and vocational interests, with special emphasis devoted to their real-world significance and their developmental antecedents. Topics of interest include educational, interpersonal, and vocational behaviours, especially those relevant to facilitating optimal adjustment to life and work and tailoring opportunities for positive growth.[6]

Of all the tests used in differential psychology, tests of *intelligence* are best known and probably most used (and abused). The history of tests of intelligence goes back to Alfred Binet (1857–1911), who invented the first modern-format intelligence test; and to Charles Spearman (1863–1945), who invented a statistical tool (factor analysis) for the hypothesis that a general mental ability ('general intelligence' or 'g') underlies all actions that require mental effort. This is defined, nowadays, as follows:

> General intelligence is ... the covariation cutting across various problem solving mediums (numerical, pictorial, verbal), assessment modalities (group, individual), and populations (cross culturally); it reflects the general factor – or commonality – shared by these multiple operations.[7]

Before Binet's and Spearman's contributions, Herbert Spencer (1820–1903) and Francis Galton (1822–1911) laid the tracks for *empirical* psychology, or the scientific study of individual differences. From these not so humble beginnings grew the field now so central to all aspects of our lives.[8]

It is interesting to note that very little has changed in terms of either the form or content of intelligence testing, apart from the really enormous amount of

---

[5] Lubinski, D., 'Scientific and social significance of assessing individual differences: "Sinking shafts at a few critical points"', *Annual Review of Psychology*, 51 (2000), 405–44.
[6] *Ibid.*, 406.
[7] *Ibid.*, 410.
[8] Cf. Deary, I.J., 'Individual differences in cognition: British contributions over a century', *British Journal of Psychology*, 92 (2001), 217–37; and Jensen, A.R., *The G Factor. The Science of Mental Ability* (London: Praeger, 1998) for an elaboration of this history.

research into, and ongoing debates about, the central construct – intelligence – and the more recent proliferation of different views on, and various models of, all kinds of intelligence.[9] It is worth noting the existing consensus regarding IQ-type tests: that our human, mental abilities are well described by a hierarchical scheme, which includes a general level of intelligence ('g'), group factors, and specific aspects of group factors.[10] Furthermore, Deary and Caryl have this to say about the agreements regarding IQ-type tests:

> ... the predictive validity of IQ-type test differences is well established. An expert Task Force ... chaired by the distinguished cognitive psychologist Ulric Neisser, was convened by the American Psychological Association in response to the furore about IQ in the wake of *The Bell Curve* ... They concluded that human intelligence differences: (1) can be measured with high reliability; and (2) are stable across most of the lifespan; (3) are significant predictors of important life outcomes; and (4) are substantially, but by no means wholly, heritable.[11]

These four points are well worth noting; so too are the reasons why IQ-type or intelligence tests are controversial. If a substantial portion of intelligence is inherited (4), it makes people fear that it is thus outside of individual or educational control; and if important parts of our lives are dependent on how clever we are, it further underlines that old, old fear that those who have much will obtain even more, and those who start off with little, will lose even what little they have. It is then 'human, all too human' to want to discredit the tests, but perhaps we need to think more cleverly about the intelligence differences between us.

It is good to remind ourselves that plus/minus 80% of people are intelligent enough – if we take the distribution of (measured) intelligence in the

[9] Cf. Carroll, J.B., *Human Cognitive Abilities. A Survey of Factor Analytic Studies* (Cambridge: CUP, 1993); Deary, I.J. and Caryl, P.G., 'Neuroscience and human intelligence', *Trends in Neuroscience*, 20/8 (1998), 365–71; Gardner, H., *Creating Minds* (New York: Basic Books, 1993); Stankov, L., 'The theory of fluid and crystallized intelligence. New findings and recent developments', *Learning and Individual Differences*, 12/1 (2000), 1–3; and Sternberg, R., *The Triarchic Mind. A New Theory of Intelligence* (New York: Viking Press, 1988).
[10] Cf. Carroll, *Human Cognitive Abilities*.
[11] Deary and Caryl, 'Neuroscience and human intelligence'.

population to include 67% of people around the mean, mode and median – for the normal run of things. My point is that most individuals, the very target of mass education, are well within an intellectual range of abilities that make them fit for schooling. Moreover, it is also such differences in intelligence as certainly exist among us that make it imperative that whatever is done in the classroom is done *well*; and it seems obvious that this is possible to the degree that the focus of the curriculum is clear, and to the degree that there are as few distractions from the curriculum as possible. All irrelevant, perhaps personal or group-specific concerns[12] can only serve to water down the time and other resources spent on equipping learners with control over the code.

Apart from differences in intelligence, rapid change and mobility across borders also mean differences in *interests* may divide a classroom. Typically, interests become the focus of psychological tests for predicting vocational paths and advising and counselling students regarding educational choice. A frequently used model of interests is that designed by Holland, which theorises how people approach and operate within learning and work environments. This model is defined by six themes, as follows:

> RIASEC: *r*ealistic [working with things and gadgets], *i*nvestigative [scientific pursuits], *a*rtistic [aesthetic pursuits and opportunities for self-expression], *s*ocial [people contact and helping professions], *e*nterprising [corporate environments: buying, marketing, selling], and *c*onventional [office practices and well-structured tasks].[13]

Unlike tests of intelligence, the assessment of interests often encounters large sex differences in individuals' test performance, with females typically veering towards 'people' (rather than 'things') in their interests. Apart from some criticism of this model, and the exclusion of specific interests such as religiosity,

---

[12] For example, something like the following: 'This course, which is (somewhat awkwardly) titled Class, Race, and Gender in the History of U.S. Education, reflects my strong belief in the need for a historical perspective for prospective teachers. It introduces prospective teachers to the powerful history of students and teachers who have claimed a broad and challenging education as a right for all people'; http://www.findarticles.com/p/articles/mi_m0JVP/is_2002_Winter/ai_97483140 .
[13] Quoted in Lubinski, 'Scientific and social significance of assessing individual differences', 425.

the RIASEC model is probably the best representation of what the assessment of interests aims at.

Another kind of psychological test comes in the form of the so-called 'Big Five' assessment of *personality* differences.[14] 'Personality' is regarded as the enduring features of someone's psychological make-up, character, or traits. In this regard, the so-called Big Five include the following features: extraversion, neuroticism, agreeableness, conscientiousness, and openness. Through testing, each individual is placed on a grid defined by the five traits. Some theorists add evaluative traits to this list, while others shorten it, or argue *against* this intra-psychic conception of personality, and for a situation-specific view of behaviour. Yet others take the defining issue of personality to be the interaction between the full constellation of characteristics.[15] I leave these tests and their uses at that, even though teachers are certainly meant to take this kind of difference also into account in their handling of individuals.

In all cases of the assessment of abilities, interests and personality, the point is to *describe* an individual's current functioning in terms of what was measured against the *norms* for the relevant group or ability, etc., so as to *predict* future possibilities. The question that has to be asked about any or all of these assessments is: do the tests furnish truthful (reliable and valid) answers? In other words, do these assessments deliver any more than common sense would? These questions are important, in that tests and their results have many and varied implications for the life-course of the individual assessed.

From the beginning of the 20th century until now, the psychology of individual differences has embodied a distinct component of empirical psychology, while providing education with evidential support for its claim to

---

[14] Cf. Funder, D.C., 'Personality', *Annual Review of Psychology*, 52 (2001), 197–221; and Paunonen, S.V. and Ashton, M.C., 'Big five factors and facets and the prediction of behaviour', *Journal of Personality and Social Psychology*, 81/3 (2001), 524–39.
[15] Cf. Eysenck, H.J., *The Structure of Human Personality* (New York: Wiley, 1953); Hogan, R. and Roberts, B.W., 'Personality measurement and employment decisions', *American Psychologists* 51/2 (1996), 469–77; and Mischel, W., *Personality and Assessment* (New York: Wiley, 1968).

know learners' abilities, interests and personalities. Yet, it must be noted that all psychological tests (unlike, say, a thermostat) fail to give results that are 100% true (reliable and valid) over time and across different situations. Further, tests exclude many facets of a life or do not encompass all there is to know, and thus often fail to predict perfectly the future successes and failures of a particular individual. How often does one hear stories of this ilk: 'The psychologist told us she would never manage this course/further education ... and look at her now: Chief Medical Officer at her hospital'. Moreover, it is prudent to acknowledge that not all tests are created equal; I thus conclude this section with some notes on the uses and abuses of tests.

The first, most obvious, abuse of tests and their results has to do with overextending a particular test's descriptive, explanatory and predictive scope. Phrased differently, all professionally developed tests are hemmed in by factors such as: the explicitly formulated purpose and scope of the tests, the population aimed at, and the limits on the measurement undertaken. Furthermore, the theoretical background to the test in question and the operationalisation of central concepts, as well as the chosen norm-group, the scientific standing of the given norms, and therefore the limits on the interpretation of test results and the reliability and validity of the test, are all crucial issues to consider. Crudely put, measures on a test of *interest* are not indicative of *intelligence*; and one standardised on 20-year-old, English-speaking males in the USA is not suitable for 50-year-old women in Africa. If whatever is measured is defined one way (e.g. intelligence = speed with which multiplications by 13 from 1–26 can be executed), then it does *not* include another way of defining intelligence (e.g. intelligence = abstract reasoning skills). Moreover, if one or the other of the constructs central to the test depends on a discarded or discredited theory (of intelligence, in our example), then the measure of this, and the test itself, are both questionable. Lastly, we expect from our tests that they will measure whatever it is that they purport to measure in the same way over repeated measures (indicative of reliability) and do so accurately (indicative of validity). Different kinds of validity, furthermore, involve the central construct measured (e.g. how well intelligence, as such, is measured), relate the parts of the test to one another and to the whole, and link the test score to 'real-life' performance, or to one or the other criterion measure.

A test that meets these criteria is not only a trustworthy instrument, but also one that has a specific – explicitly stated – scope, which must be taken seriously by those who will use the test and interpret the results. Even the best tool can be turned into a useless instrument if a clumsy or stupid agent should misapply it. In this regard it is often not so much the tests that fail us, as the practitioner's over-hasty and careless jump from a test score to a set of recommendations. Take, for example, a score on an IQ test of 85: if one wanted to be 100% sure that one had the correct measure of the person's intellectual abilities (scientifically justifiable conclusions regarding the measurement of an individual's performance on various test items, in terms of a specified norm group, etc.), one would have to say that a person who scored thus had an IQ in *the range* of 70–100, give or take five points at both ends to allow for different scoring systems. If we think of a *range* of possible scores, of which the given score (85 in our example) is the mid-point, the individual's abilities begin to look both more flexible (their expression perhaps depending on context and learning opportunities) and not as clearly pinned to *one*, and only one, point on a scale. The fact is, though, that we rarely think of such a range of possibilities, and tend to regard the actual point as a fixed, an absolute, indication of intelligence, and make our recommendations accordingly. But this is to abuse testing and any particular test of intelligence.

The abuses of tests most typically involve violating the scientific framework of the test in question, and practitioners not keeping to the rules of scientific practice: the rules being, for example, upholding the set, standardised procedure for administering the test; being objective in scoring; remaining within the limits of the test's construction framework for the interpretation of results; and basing recommendations solely on the scope outlined in the test manual. The responsible use of tests thus demands that users of tests familiarise themselves with the critical literature surrounding any particular test. This again underlines the approach to knowledge advocated in Chapter 2: (a) reading and thinking about problems hypothetically, i.e. as if answers are not ready-made but possible in view of the best knowledge on a problem; (b) searching for answers with the most empirical and logical support; (c) comparing the selected answers against each other and against their respective outcomes in particular situations; and (d) continuing to search for possible answers through *hypothetical thinking* about the problems in the classroom.

Another side to the story about testing has to do with the life circumstances of individuals or groups; that is, their learning opportunities, access to resources, exposure to stimuli, and health and nutritional background *before*, and up to, the testing occasion. For example, someone who has never encountered various gadgets or corporate environments cannot express these interests on a test of interest. If such a person is, however, exposed to such opportunities *during* testing, or *in between* testing occasions, she may well develop these interests. This is the issue behind the much-vaunted dynamic paradigm in testing, or tests of potential.[16] This issue has a specific bite when it comes to disadvantaged populations and individuals who have, for various socio-economic or other reasons, been denied the relevant opportunities to operate like their peers as far as their abilities, interests and personalities go. It was in response to this situation in South Africa that the Teach-Test-Teach (TTT) programme, referred to in Chapter 1, was undertaken. Part of the aim of this intervention was – in the absence of either useful psychometric data or school test-results – to find empirically sound

---

[16] Cf. Grigorenko, E.L. and Sternberg, R.J., 'Dynamic testing', *Psychological Bulletin*, 124/1 (1998), 75–111; Hamers, J.H.M., Sijtsma, K. and Riujssenaars, A.J.J.M., *Learning Potential Assessment. Theoretical, Methodological and Practical Issues* (Amsterdam: Swets and Zeitlinger, 1993); and Luther, M., Cole, E. and Gamlin, P., *Dynamic Assessment for Instruction. From Theory to Application* (York, CA: Captus University Press, 1996).

indices of applicants' (admitted to a two-week assessment programme) ability to benefit from and contribute to university studies, or of their 'potential' to learn.

The notion of assessing *potential* comes from Feuerstein's work,[17] as already noted, and uses Vygotsky's ideas about the ZPD[18] as a framework for devising a suitable dynamic test. This involves measures of: (a) learners' actual development or the performances they can produce unassisted, (b) performances learners can produce through assistance/under guidance, and (c) the distance between (a) and (b).[19] Moreover, it is thought that this is a better way of predicting future behaviour (or of doing so more accurately than through static tests) in cases where learners have lacked certain opportunities for learning *before* the (static) test. It is thus crucial in assessments of potential or in dynamic testing to ask and determine the necessary training/teaching to be included before or during testing.

The *reasons* for or *causes* of learners' poor performances or low scores on various school tasks, tests and ability measures, and learning difficulties, in general, are thus important for directing intervention (teaching and testing) in the assessment of potential. For example, if a learner's reading age is below what is expected for his age, and the cause of this is lack of familiarity with the alphabet, then it is the latter that becomes the target for intervention. In this sense, the reasons for or causes of a big gap between actual and potential performance on

---

[17] Feuerstein, R., *The Dynamic Assessment of Retarded Performers* (Baltimore: University Park Press, 1979); and Feuerstein, R., Rand, Y., Hoffman, M.B. and Miller, R., *Instrumental Enrichment. An Intervention Program for Cognitive Modifiability* (Baltimore: University Park Press, 1980).

[18] In Vygotsky's own words: 'The ZPD defines those functions that have not yet matured but are in the process of maturation, functions that will mature tomorrow but are currently in an embryonic state. These functions could be termed the "buds" or "flowers" of development rather than the "fruits" of development'; Vygotsky, L.S., *Mind in Society. The Development of Higher Psychological Processes*, Cole, M., John-Steiner, V., Scribner, S. and Souberman, E. (eds.) (Cambridge, MA: Harvard University Press, 1978), 84.

[19] For Vygotsky, the ZPD is a model of the difference between 'development' and 'learning', or the difference between that which unfolds spontaneously and that which can deliberately be brought into the ambit of the child through teaching-learning; and it is a model for enculturation through communication. It is *not* specifically a model for the remediation of learning difficulties and under-preparedness; this aim is added by Feuerstein and, through his clinical work, ideas about 'cultural deprivation', and programmes for instrumental enrichment, which more or less rely on some of Vygotsky's ideas about learning and development.

122

some or other task, or measure of learning, draw intelligence, interest, personality and also cultural differences into the discussion.

Typically, then, in an attempt to measure the distance between unassisted and assisted performance on some set of tasks, the dynamic framework is opposed to conventional, static testing such as standard IQ-type tests. At best, I would argue, the purpose of this *kind* of assessment (i.e. dynamic assessment) is to:

- *quantify intra-individual change* (or to capture, empirically and statistically, the 'learning-curve' of each individual); and

- *predict future performance* more accurately than could be achieved through a conventional test in cases where obtaining reliable and valid measures of an individual/group is problematic for whatever reason.

The achievement of these objectives in an *economical way* (i.e. in terms of time, money, teaching and other resources) depends very much on the kind of research undertaken in order to determine the kind of experiences or learning opportunities to include as part of the dynamic testing situation. The practical implications of opting for a dynamic model of testing have to do with deciding how 'dynamic' the stituation is to be. For example, one may choose the 'within-test-training' framework, or ongoing cycles of intervention (either test-teach-test, or teach-test-teach), each with different resource implications.

It is interesting to note at this point that *the normal process of education (with its cycles of teaching and testing, measures of school performance, and additional psychometric measures) is, in fact, a form of dynamic testing.* That is to say, the ongoing cycles of teaching and testing that characterise schooling (including teaching aimed at certain objectives as contained in a particular curriculum) represent a long-term dynamic testing situation. The point is that when we think of 'dynamic testing' as a specific *kind* of test,[20] one aimed at

---

[20] A kind of testing that aims at the *processes* involved in learning (not the products only), that involves *feedback* to the learner regarding his/her performance, and that depends on a two-way interactive relationship between tester and testee (cf. Grigorenko and Sternberg, 'Dynamic testing', 75).

learners with a big enough gap (e.g. between their actual and potential development) to warrant a Learning Potential (LP) intervention, we want to design teaching-testing cycles somewhere short of the long-term situation.

The difficult empirical matter is thus to determine how many (and what kind of) assessments and interventions to include (i.e. the form and content[21] to focus the training during or before re-testing, as well as the testing, on), in order to provide good strong data for diagnosis, ongoing intervention, and prediction.[22] We may also note, for what it is worth, that dynamic assessments are less inclined than the other kinds of tests introduced above to attempt to *find* and *fix* something 'inside' the individual; and, as such, therefore, dynamic assessments better fit the newer kinds of thinking about cognition.

If indeed cognition (thinking, problem-solving and so on) breaks through the boundaries of skin and skull, and draws on resources in the social and material world around us, as Andy Clark and others emphasise, then the differences between us take on a far less inner, mental tenor (see Chapter 3, above). The downside of this view of cognition for education is that those who have access to *knowledge-rich* artefacts and technologies are also cognitively better off in most global sites of exchange than the rest. This, then, shows how a distributed view of cognition draws us close to the political problems related to the distribution of resources. As stated in Chapter 1, it is the consequences of unequal access to relevant resources that brought me into the study of cognition but, more importantly for our purposes, it is this situation that increasingly defines central problems for education, globally. It is also the consequences of the unequal

---

[21] In general, Feuerstein's own work only remediates cognitive operations, thus only focuses on form; during the TTT programme already referred to, we included both, and thus designed a set of learning materials to capture the necessary *content* demands of tasks as well as the *form* of these; see Craig, A.P. and Bradbury, J.L., *A Guide to Learning* (Kenwyn: Juta and Co. Ltd, 1994).

[22] Cf. Craig, A.P., 'Time and learning', *South African Journal of Psychology*, 30/4 (2000), 6–16; Craig, A.P., 'Education for all', *South African Journal of Higher Education*, 10/2 (1996), 47–55; and Craig, A.P., 'The conflict between the familiar and the unfamiliar', *South African Journal of Higher Education*, 3/1 (1989), 166–72.

124

distribution of resources that underlie my reasoning about equipping the least advantaged with the winning skills, technologies and knowledge in the classroom.

5.2 Culture and change

Luria wrote, early on in the 20th century, that:

> It seems surprising that the science of psychology has avoided the idea that mental processes are social and historical in origin, or that important manifestations of human consciousness have been directly shaped by the basic practices of human activity and the actual forms of life.[23]

This is no longer ignored, as we saw in Chapter 3; but this does not mean that there are no debates about the implications of cultural or group differences. On the one hand, there is a clamour to recognise and acknowledge these differences and, on the other, every attempt is made to underplay or deny differences. It is, for example, acceptable to claim special interests and protection and so on for particular groups; but not at all acceptable to state that this group lacks this or that ability, that the social and material world of some people equips them better for certain skills than others, and that they are thus less able to fulfil positions that demand the skills their experiences do not prepare them for.

In learning to survive and even thrive in a particular eco-cultural niche, we, like other animals, come to act and react in discernible and context-appropriate ways. The cultures we thus make and live by include tasks with their own histories or place in 'our' culture. For example, to learn to track animal spoor in the desert, or to learn to surf the web on a computer, define two quite different 'proper contexts' or homes.[24] If and when such different realities meet or come into conflict in the marketplace of skills exchange, or in the classroom, one rather than the other group will be disadvantaged given the demands of the tasks

---

[23] Luria, A.R., *Cognitive Development: Its Cultural and Social Foundations* (Cambridge, MA: Harvard University Press, 1976), 3.
[24] See Clark's discussion of the tuna; Clark, A., 'Where brain, body, and world collide', *Cognitive Systems Research*, 1/1 (1999), 10.

favoured in that marketplace or classroom. This surely is Luria's point, which emphasises not only differences between cultures and the relationship between mind and culture, but also differences in the tasks typical of one world, and the skills, technology, and knowledge this world and its typical tasks imply and embody.[25] This becomes a difficult educational – if not also a political – problem, when a specific context demands or favours one set of skills, and not others (e.g. undertaking a web search versus tracking animal spoor). It is at this point that the call to relativism is most strongly felt by some, but this is hardly a responsible move – educationally speaking – as already argued.[26]

Generally, one of the following is typically proposed when people from one culture (and its skills, technology and knowledge) come into an alien or new situation typified by unfamiliar tasks:

- Furnish the neophyte with the new skills, technology and knowledge demanded by the unfamiliar task;[27]
- Change the situation;[28]
- Ignore the differences or treat the task *as if* it is similar to, or the same as, familiar tasks.

It is primarily the first response, involving changing the habitual repertoire of the learner, that I want to discuss below. The second option, i.e. where the situation is changed, represents an interesting case of *deliberate transformation*, but less interesting as far as differences in the classroom go. To change the situation in cases where there is a mismatch between individual skills and knowledge and the

---

[25] Cf. Cole, M. and Scribner, S., *Culture and Thought: A Psychological Introduction* (New York: John Wiley and Sons, Inc., 1974); Craig, 'Time and learning', 6–16; D'Andrade, R.G., 'The cultural part of cognition', *Cognitive Science*, 5 (1981), 179–95; Feuerstein, Rand, Hoffman and Miller, *Instrumental Enrichment*; Valsiner, J., *Culture and Human Development: An Introduction* (London: Sage, 2000); Vygotsky, *Mind in Society*; and Wertsch, J., *Culture, Communication and Cognition* (Cambridge: CUP, 1985).

[26] To overcome this kind of conflict *politically* is another matter: force the *direction* of change violently or through other less offensive means.

[27] Cf. Morphet, T., Lazarus, J. and Hunter, P., 'General conclusion', *South African Journal of Higher Education*, 3/1 (1989), 172.

[28] Cf. Kirsh, D., 'Adapting the environment instead of oneself', *Adaptive Behavior*, 4/3/4 (1996), 415–52.

cognitive demands of a task, is rare because it requires that the group, individual, or both *recognise* the mismatch as well as the *nature* of this and, in addition, have the wherewithal to *change* the task to suit their own skills and knowledge. This is already to go beyond the task at hand. It is however the pot of gold at the end of the educational rainbow. That is to say, such *deliberate transformation* can certainly be hoped for *after* schooling from those with control over the code. Asking of pupils deliberate transformation *during* their schooling is possibly not feasible. In addition, such an imposition might be tantamount to robbing them of the necessary care and responsibility of adults, as Hannah Arendt pointed out (see Chapter 1).

The third option – treating the task *as if* it is familiar – constitutes what could be called a 'common-sense appropriation' of alien things; but crucial to note is that this will happen at the cost of change and adaptation in both senses discussed here. Were this to happen invariably and everywhere, we might still be hunting and gathering! To put it more formally, it is our very human nature to make unfamiliar tasks, situations, and territories our own. Moreover, it is this adeptness on which we pin our hopes for progress, in general, and the success of education in particular. It is therefore strange that so much ink (and blood) is spilled on trying to prevent change. More particularly, demands for relevance in education (i.e. to bring familiar tasks to the classroom), relativism about knowledge (i.e. to underline the strong relationship between context and belief), and fears about domination of one set of beliefs over another in the market place of skills exchange, seem to go against our natural abilities to change. They also seem to me to be attempts to lock people into their cultural posts.

For a group to want to hang onto their special or unique form of dress, eating habits, gods, and other ideas is unproblematic; when it comes to wanting to draw *limits* around 'their' (own) intelligence, the issue is murkier. A theorist like Ogbu, for example, maintains that children are socialised to acquire those skills that will ensure their successful integration into their group of *origin* and that this means, for him, that 'to be intelligent' in one versus another group or context will not be the same.[29] He defines 'intelligence', from a cross-cultural perspective, thus: 'intelligence is a cultural system of thought, a cultural or group's repertoire of adaptive intellectual (or cognitive) skills'.[30] This is fine as far as it goes – but it does not go very far now, does it?

It is obvious, uncontroversial, and tautological that specific cultural ways prepare members for culturally specific ways. But, as we noted above regarding intelligence, and as argued in the previous chapter on the study of cognition, we are also creatures who share a universal *biological* history, which imposes certain *constraints* on what we do (including how we are intelligent in particular contexts), as this history also defines a certain *human* nature. It is thus the shared abilities and capacities that make change, adaptation and communication in general possible. And it is our shared humanity that balks at limited and limiting views on intelligence; these are useless in the very situations where we most need an answer to the following Big Question: Can we change? Or are we *locked* into our cultural posts?

Moreover, Ogbu's attempt to put a positive spin on cultural differences skirts the really hard question for education: what if particular 'cultural ways' ill prepare some people for valued skills, technology and knowledge? His kind of relativism thus does not get us out of the deep water when having to think of ways of bringing different histories together in one place, i.e. the classroom. Moreover, it is this kind of thinking that led to a policy such as apartheid in South Africa. It is not often enough recognised that 'apartheid' – or the policy of *separate* development for *different* people (separated according to some set of criteria defining both differences between, and similarities within, groups) – is in principle no different, and to me no more offensive, than promoting special forms

[29] Ogbu, J.U. and Stern, P., 'Caste status and intellectual development', in Sternberg, R.J. and Grigorenko, E.L. (eds.), *Environmental Effects on Cognitive Abilities* (New Jersey: Lawrence Erlbaum Associates, Inc., 1994), 1–37; and Ogbu, J.U., 'Origins of human competence: A cultural-ecological perspective', *Child Development*, 52 (1981), 413–29.
[30] *Ibid.*, 5.

128

of education for particular groups, e.g. for women, Africans, or any other group thought to be maligned or discriminated against by a *universal* focus. This outlines another set of reasons behind wanting to find a central focus for schooling – albeit that my viewpoint necessitates addressing differences in the classroom, rather than side-stepping them as Ogbu and all relativistic thinking try to do.

If schooling is to deliver a globally competitive, technologically skilled and knowledgeable population, relativistic talk is useless. I thus want to underline the argument pursued in different terms in the previous chapters; that mass schooling, movement across porous national and other boundaries, and the fact of increasing universal standardisation, make it imperative that schooling equips learners with control over the code. As such, changing both the habitual repertoire of learners participating in schooling, and the tasks that define this shared learning environment, seem to me both uncontroversial and crucially focused on the question about the differences between us. A related empirical matter has to do with how far such change is possible or whether there are critical ages and stages for adapting to school tasks, beyond which change will be too disruptive, unpleasant, or difficult.

To repeat a point made earlier: I think it safe to say that schooling occurs throughout the life-stages or ages during which one need not fear damage due to learning new ways of thinking, doing, and knowing. If damage *does* result during schooling, the chances are much greater that this is the result of *not* coping cognitively and/or culturally. And it is by way of finding remedies for the latter that I introduce a framework, below, for the study of differences in the classroom.

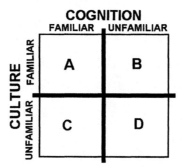

Figure 1: Classification of Tasks

In the classification of tasks in Figure 1, note that a task may be: *cognitively* familiar or unfamiliar, the former having to do with the spontaneous application of existing knowledge and skills, or the exercise of the habitual repertoire; this will be experienced as doing something naturally, without conscious effort. Tasks that are cognitively unfamiliar are typical of new tasks introduced in the curriculum, or tasks of greater complexity further up the school grades. Tasks that are *culturally* familiar are part of the relevant groups' normal socialisation or reality, while culturally unfamiliar tasks are regarded as not part of 'our' way of living, or thinking, knowing and doing.

When a task is *both culturally and cognitively unfamiliar* – a situation that epitomises the most arduous learning situation, as noted in Chapter 1 – educational intervention of a very specific kind is crucial. Otherwise, the learner is left without the spontaneous guidance of the older generation or the group as a whole, in addition to having to struggle along with the rest of his people/group for access to the new skills, technology and knowledge. A task that is mixed – in the sense of being cognitively familiar (i.e. within the normal age-capacities of an individual) but culturally unfamiliar – requires minimal *personal* change. And, when the task is cognitively unfamiliar but culturally familiar, it means that the individual can rely on the resources of the group as a whole to overcome the gap

130

between what she knows and can do spontaneously, and what the new task demands.

Each of the situations clarified above in terms of the classification of tasks, captures a different educational load regarding the demands on the individual versus the group. In addition, each category requires something else from the teacher if learning is to occur. The classification and the elaboration of learning-teaching demands seems to me a more productive framework for understanding the cognitive and learning problems Feuerstein attributes to a lack of, or poor quality, MLE.[31] That is to say: individuals trapped *outside* the new (for lack of adequate induction into the demands of the new), and without the guidance of their cultural group as a whole, or without the support of their taken-for-granted ways (i.e. those that define them as a group), will tend to show impaired cognitive functioning. The reason for the latter is, however, more adequately captured by thinking of individuals in this situation as lacking opportunities and resources for acquiring, adapting to, or learning new tasks and their unfamiliar demands, than as lacking MLE *per se*.

Apart from indicating specific empirical work to be undertaken by the light of cognitive science, the framework presented in Figure 1 also provides the teacher with a handy tool for examining *what* has to be taught and to *whom* in any particular situation. More particularly, and as noted about the assessment of learning potential, this kind of *focused* education will close the gap between the newcomers' habitual performances and the demands of unfamiliar tasks. Phrased differently, education is focused through intervention aimed at a specified *form* (cognitive operations) and (curriculum) *content*; and the gap is closed when the newcomers' performance in new situations meet the demands of the tasks typical of these unfamiliar situations.[32] And I repeat: in assisting with providing more focused education, the framework guides further research – research aimed at

[31] Feuerstein, *The Dynamic Assessment of Retarded Performers*; and Feuerstein, Rand, Hoffman and Miller, *Instrumental Enrichment*.
[32] Cf. Craig, 'Education for all'.

structuring and scheduling learning opportunities in classrooms characterised by the kind of differences discussed in this chapter.

From this section and the framework above, it should be clear that the habitual repertoire of a learner may be more or less suitable for a given task; and, moreover, that a group's experiences, or eco-cultural niche, will be either more or less enabling in the case of new or unfamiliar tasks and situations. It is thus to schooling that we must turn to overcome such gaps as exist between what is taken for granted in one context, and what we encounter in another. Overcoming such gaps is thus an *educational* task underwritten by our natures, the vigour of our intelligence, and our human ability to change. The latter seems to me already enough to proceed with the urgent task of enabling all people, everywhere, with the wherewithal to engage and cope successfully with what is on offer, and at best, to make the future a better place for all.

5.3 Three theses about learning

Learning is ubiquitous unless blocked

We considered individual (intelligence, interest, and personality) differences, as well as cultural differences, above. Obviously there are also other blocks to learning. The point of this thesis is to re-focus the attention of teachers on what *prevents* a process that is a natural part of our species: *learning and change*. Moreover, all people share capacities (e.g. consciousness, the ability to reflect and reflect on their reflections, or to cognise in general) and abilities (e.g. memory and language). In addition, we can be certain that the evidence about our differences (regarding most of the things we value) tends to point towards greater *intra*-group differences than *inter*-group differences, which means it is highly contentious to talk about women, or some particular group's way of thinking, knowing, etc. as irredeemably different from the rest, as argued elsewhere.[33] It is still worthwhile to

---

[33] Craig, A.P., 'Culture and knowledge', *South African Journal of Philosophy*, 20/2 (2001), 204.

132

repeat the point, made in Chapter 2, that the facts of change, adaptation and communication undermine drawing strong or inevitable links between culture and knowledge. These facts also underline our common, human nature and the fact that each of us is already multicultural (except in rare cases of imposed isolation).[34]

Learning new ways of thinking, acting, knowing and so on should therefore be expected as a normal outcome of living and any part of this, such as schooling. When learning does *not* happen, it becomes a matter for applied cognition, i.e. turning the best of cognitive science into hypotheses for investigating why it does/did not occur.

Biology (brains and bodies) directs the course of learning
In Chapter 3 I gave Andy Clark's work quite an airing because I think his model of us as natural-born cyborgs, as well as a view of cognition as distributed, holds out interesting possibilities for the classroom (obviously at best as *hypotheses* for empirical scrutiny in particular situations).[35] For one thing, it de-emphasises what is 'inside' in favour of what is *between* and *around* people – thus shifting the attention in the classroom to what could augment and enhance our natural abilities or functions; for example, determining just how pupils could be taught to use the external environment as a resource of 'cognition-enhancing "wideware"'.[36]

The more conventional view of the manner in which our biology is implicated in learning has to do with Seligman's notion of 'prepared learning' i.e.

---

[34] Cf. Craig, A.P., 'Culture and the individual', *Theory and Psychology*, 13/5 (2003).
[35] I happen to think that it is not all as easy as Clark makes out; for one thing, I do not understand the mechanisms whereby very different kinds of things such as human brains can enter 'into an increasingly potent cascade of genuinely symbiotic relationships with knowledge-rich artefacts and technologies' – unless this merely means we use whatever we can lay our hands on, that we are tool-makers and users, as the old story goes; see Clark, A., *Being There. Putting Brain, Body, and World Together Again* (Cambridge, MA: The MIT Press, 1999), 2.
[36] Clark clarifies 'wideware' as follows: external items (devices, media, notations that scaffold and *complement* but usually do not replicate) biological modes of computation and processing, creating extended cognitive systems whose computational profiles are quite different from those of the isolated brain'; *Idem*.

133

'that animals and humans are innately prepared to learn certain behaviours, while being counterprepared against – that is, predisposed to avoid – others'.[37] This is a further pointer to our *nature*, what we bring to learning, or innate constraints on learning.[38] This approach clearly suggests interesting empirical projects around the difficulties experienced by most learners on some tasks (e.g. mathematics) while not on others (e.g. mother tongue or second language learning early on in development). Finding ways to utilise what we are (biologically) prepared for – in order to teach what we find difficult – or perhaps, specifically, trying to find ways to go against the grain, promises exciting research and possibilities for intervening in the classroom and on the street.

Context exploits and/or limits our plasticity
As far as the limiting effects of particular contexts go, we have discussed culture, opportunities for learning, and access to resources. What deserves considerable emphasis is that increasingly we think of context all the way back to the pre-birth environment of an individual, and the longer genetic history of her biology. Thus, for instance, the consequences of poverty (e.g. malnutrition) are not innocent of significant differences in the classroom. Further, it is salutary to be reminded of the way what is around people influences their achievements.

Lloyd's ongoing analyses of, and comparison between, Greek and other ancient societies such as China for the roots of scientific and philosophical

---

[37] Wilson, E.O., *Consilience. The Unity of Knowledge* (London: Abacus, 1998), 165.
[38] See Cummins, D.D. and Cummins, R., 'Biological preparedness and evolutionary explanation', *Cognition*, 73/3 (1999), 37–53, for a description of the following: 'There are neurological biases present at birth, and these are the result of millions of years of evolution operating on the ontogeny of the modern mammalian brain. This means that the developing brain is not entirely plastic ... the infant mind is cognitively predisposed to interpret the world in terms of agents and objects ... With respect to agents, they appreciate the inherently reciprocal nature of social interactions ... and the meaning of emotional facial expressions ... With respect to objects, they appreciate that objects are permanent entities that cannot occupy the same space at the same time ... whose movements are constrained by physical causality ... and principles of biomechanical movement ... They also appreciate the abstract concept of number and arithmetic operations (43).

134

thinking[39] adds an interesting dimension to the view of cognition as embedded in a context. Lloyd is at pains to point out that there are no grounds for believing in a 'Greek miracle,' nor in some specific 'Greek mentality' that could be advanced to explain the development of scientific and philosophical thinking from roughly five centuries before the Common Era. Rather, as he shows, these modes of thought and interpersonal interactions sprang from a number of socio-political factors. He writes:

> In the admittedly speculative business of attempting to elucidate why it was that certain kinds of intellectual inquiry came to be initiated in ancient Greece, we must first take stock of certain of the economic, technological and other factors ... affecting not only Greece itself, but also one or more of her ancient Near Eastern neighbours ...[40]

These economic, technological and other factors were, according to Lloyd:

- The existence of an economic surplus and of money as a medium of exchange;
- Access to, and curiosity about, other societies; and
- Changes in the technical means of communication and the beginnings of literacy.

Lloyd thus emphasises the interaction between *political* (and, one could add, the economic consequences of this), and *intellectual* experiences. He writes about this as follows:

> Ancient Greece is marked not just by exceptional intellectual developments, but also by what is in certain respects an exceptional political situation: and the two appear to be connected. In four fundamental ways aspects of Greek political experience may be thought either to have directly influenced, or to be closely mirrored in, key features of the intellectual developments we are concerned with. First, there is the possibility of radical innovation, second the openness of access to the forum of debate, third the habit of scrutiny, and

---

[39] Thinking committed to demonstration through evidence and argument. See Lloyd, G.E.R. *Adversaries and Authorities* (Cambridge: CUP, 1996); Lloyd, G.E.R., *Demystifying Mentalities* (Cambridge: CUP, 1990); Lloyd, G.E.R., *The Revolutions of Wisdom* (Berkeley: Berkeley University Press 1987); Lloyd, G.E.R., *Magic, Reason and Experience* (Cambridge: CUP, 1979); and Lloyd, G.E.R., *Polarity and Analogy* (Cambridge: CUP, 1966).
[40] Lloyd, *Magic, Reason and Experience*, 258.

fourth the expectation of justification – giving an account – and the premium set on rational methods of doing so.[41]

To repeat these distinctive factors about ancient Greek society or the intellectual climate of the time: the possibility of radical innovation; access to the forum(s) of debate; the habit of scrutiny; and the expectation of justification.

If Lloyd is right that what underwrote the so-called 'Greek Miracle' was the *interaction* between specific economic, technological and other factors, and thus a certain intellectual climate, then there is more to worry about in Clark's view that '… the world of artefacts, texts, media, and even cultural practices and institutions, might be for us what the actively created whorls and vortices are for the Bluefin tuna'.[42] And this, to emphasise a point, has enormous implications for education.

If each individual mind (and all the rest involved in cognition) grows from the world surrounding it, or the social communication between people (as Vygotsky would have it), then differences in these matter more than the issue of whether one is relativist, pluralist or even historicist about these. Moreover, it then becomes a pressing educational issue just how to enable everyone who chooses to participate in what is on offer to do so successfully; that is to say, *how to overcome differences towards equal access to and facility with the valued skills, technology and knowledge that define winning exchanges.*

In more general terms, work like Lloyd's, and in another vein Vygotsky's and Clark's, certainly highlights the manner in which what is natural or 'inside' each of us finds expression and at best enhancement through what is 'outside'

---

[41] *Idem.*

[42] Clark goes on as follows: 'Human brains, raised in this sea of cultural tools, might develop strategies for advanced problem solving that "factor in" these external resources as profoundly and deeply as the bodily motions of the tuna factor in and maximally exploit the reliable properties of the surrounding water. Recognising the complex ways in which human thought and reason exploit the presence of external symbols and problem-solving resources, and unravelling the ways in which biological brains couple themselves with these very special kinds of ecological objects, is surely one of the most exciting tasks confronting the science of embodied cognition – and one that might shed great light on the role of embodiment in more abstract cognitive domains'; Clark, A., 'An embodied cognitive science?', *Trends in Cognitive Science*, 3/9 (1999), 349.

each biological skin bag; as such, this work gives schooling a clear point over and above Mother Nature. Moreover, such views on what learning and cognition in general might involve give a very particular tone to my proposal that the excellence of mass schooling lies in equipping learners with the wherewithal to access, use and perhaps change in time what is on offer. Equipping learners with control over the code, i.e. control over universally standardised skills, technology and knowledge, education can rely on the natural, *human* ability to learn and change.

BIBLIOGRAPHY

Ainslie, G., *Breakdown of Will* (Cambridge: CUP, 2001).

Anderson, M., 'Ask not what you can do for modularity but what can modularity do for you', *Learning and Individual Differences*, 10/3 (1998), 251–7.

Ansari, D. and Coch, D., 'Bridges over troubled waters: Education and cognitive neuroscience', *Trends in Cognitive Science*, 10/4 (2006), 146–51.

Appiah, K.A. and Gutmann, A., *Color Conscious. The Political Morality of Race* (Princeton, NJ: Princeton University Press, 1996).

Arendt, H., *Between Past and Future* (London: Penguin, 1993).

Aristotle, *A Treatise on Government*, trans. W. Ellis (London: J.M. Dent and Sons Ltd, 1941).

—*The Politics of Aristotle*, trans. with notes by E. Barker (Oxford: The Clarendon Press, 1948).

—*The Nicomachean Ethics of Aristotle* (Intro. by J.A. Smith), trans. D.P. Chase (London: J.M. Dent and Sons Ltd, 1949).

Barkow, J.H., Cosmides, L. and Tooby, J., *The Adapted Mind. Evolutionary Psychology and the Generation of Culture* (Oxford: OUP, 1992).

Beer, C.G., 'Trial and errors in the evolution of cognition', *Behavioural Processes*, 35 (1996), 215–24.

Beer, R.D., 'Dynamical approaches to cognitive science', *Trends in Cognitive Science*, 4/3 (March 2000), 91–9.

Berlin, I., *Against the Current. Essays in the History of Ideas* (Intro. by R. Hausheer), Hardy, H. (ed.) (Oxford: OUP, 1981), 111–29.

—*The Crooked Timber of Humanity* (New York: Vintage Books, 1992).

—*The Roots of Romanticism* (The A.W. Mellon Lectures in the Fine Arts: The National Gallery of Art, Washington DC, Bollingen Series xxxv, 45), Hardy, H. (ed.) (Princeton, NJ: Princeton University Press, 1999).

Berk, L. and Garvin, R., 'Development of private speech among low-income Appalachian children', *Developmental Psychology*, 20/2 (1984), 271–86.

Bernstein, B., *The Structuring of Pedogogic Discourse. Volume IV. Class, Codes, and Control* (London: Routledge and Kegan Paul, 1990).

Bernstein, R.J., *Beyond Objectivism and Relativism* (Oxford: Blackwell, 1983).

Bickhard, M.H., 'The import of Fodor's anti-constructivist argument', in Steffe, L. (ed.), *Epistemological Foundations of Mathematical Experience* (New York: Springer-Verlag, 1991).

—'Commentary: On the cognition in cognitive development', *Developmental Review*, 19 (1999), 369–89.

—'A challenge to constuctivism: Internal and external sources of constructive constraint', *Human Development*, 47 (2004), 94–9.

Bickle, J. and Mandik, P., 'The philosophy of neuroscience', in Zalta, E.N. (ed.), *The Stanford Encyclopedia of Philosophy* (Winter 2002 Edition).

Bivens, J. and Berk, L., 'A longitudinal study of the development of elementary school children's private speech', *Merrill-Palmer Quarterly*, 36/4 (1990), 443–63.

Bloom, H., *The Western Canon* (London: Papermac, 1995).

—'Instant evolution. The influence of the city on human genes: A speculative case', *New Ideas in Psychology*, 19/3 (2001), 203–20.

Bodanis, D., $E=MC^2$. *A Biography of the World's Most Famous Equation* (London: Macmillan, 2000).

Booth, W., 'One nation, indivisible: Is it history?', *Washington Post* (Sunday 22 February 1998).

Bradie, M., and Harms, W., 'Evolutionary Epistemology', in Zalta, E.N. (ed.), *The Stanford Encyclopedia of Philosophy* (Spring 2004 Edition).

Caroll, J.B., *Human Cognitive Abilities. A Survey of Factor Analytic Studies* (Cambridge: CUP, 1993).

Carpendale, J.I.M. and Lewis, C., 'Constructing an understanding of mind: The development of children's social understanding within social interaction', *Behavioral and Brain Sciences*, 27 (2004), 79–151.

Case, R., *The Mind's Staircase. Exploring the Conceptual Underpinnings of Children's Thought and Knowledge* (Hillsdale, NJ: Lawrence Erlbaum Associates, Inc., 1992).

—Demetriou, A., Platsidou, M. and Kazi, S., 'Integrating concepts and tests of intelligence from the differential and developmental traditions', *Intelligence*, 29 (2001), 307–36.

Cavalli-Sforza, L.L., *Genes, People and Languages* (London: Penguin, 2001).

Chomsky, N., *Language and Mind* (New York: Harcourt, Brace and World, 1968).

—'Review of Skinner's *Verbal Behavior*', *Language*, 35 (1959), 26–58.

Churchland, P.M., *The Engine of Reason, the Seat of the Soul. A Philosophical Journey into the Brain* (Cambridge, MA: The MIT Press, 2000).

Churchland, P.S., 'How do neurons know?', *Daedalus*, Winter 2004.

Cioffi, F., *Wittgenstein on Freud and Frazer* (Cambridge: CUP, 1998).

Clark, A., *Being There. Putting Brain, Body, and World Together Again* (Cambridge, MA: The MIT Press, 1999).

—*Natural-born Cyborgs. Minds, Technologies, and the Future of Human Intelligence* (Oxford: OUP, 2003).

—'Moving minds: Situated content in the service of real-time success', *Philosophical Perspectives*, 9 (1995), 94.

—'The dynamical challenge', *Cognitive Science*, 21/4 (1997), 461–81.

—'An embodied cognitive science?', *Trends in Cognitive Science*, 3/9 (1999), 345–51.

—'Where brain, body, and world collide', *Cognitive Systems Research*, 1/1 (1999), 5–17.

—'Reasons, robots and the extended mind', *Mind and Language*, 16/2 (March 2001), 123.

Cole, M., *Cultural Psychology: A Once and Future Discipline* (Cambridge, MA: Harvard University Press, 1996).

—and Scribner, S., *Culture and Thought. A Psychological Introduction* (New York: John Wiley and Sons, Inc., 1974).

—Valsiner, J., Engelström, Y., Branco, A.U. and Vasquez, O., *Mind, Culture and Activity. Seminal Papers from the Laboratory of Comparative Human Cognition* (Cambridge: CUP, 1998).

Comte-Sponville, A., *A Short Treatise on the Great Virtues. The Uses of Philosophy in Everyday Life* (London: Vintage, 2003).

Craig, A.P., *Mothers and Children: An Analysis of Change* (Unpublished doctoral dissertation, Department of Psychology, University of Natal, Durban, 1985).

—*The Production of Knowledge* (Durban: Tegwen Publications; TTT Publications, 1988 [1989 revised]).

—'A cognitive infrastructure for change', *Theoria*, LXX (1987), 77–83.

—'Excellence in and through education', *South African Journal of Higher Education*, 2/1 (1988), 3–8.

—'On the method of analysing human transactions recorded on videotape', *South African Journal of Psychology*, 18/3 (1988), 96–103.

—'The conflict between the familiar and the unfamiliar', *South African Journal of Higher Education*, 3/1 (1989), 166–72.

—'Adult cognition and tertiary studies', *South African Journal of Higher Education*, 5/2 (1991), 137–44.

—'The study of change', in *Cognitive Development in Southern Africa*, compiled by H. van Niekerk (Pretoria: Human Sciences Research Council, 1991).

—'Education for all', *South African Journal of Higher Education*, 10/2 (1996), 47–55.

—'Really virtual/Virtually real', in Bensusan, D. (ed.), *W(h)ither the University* (Kenwyn: Juta and Co. Ltd, 1996).

—'Knowledge and democracy', *South African Journal of Higher Education*, 13/1 (1999), 18–30.

—'To live for a future', *Psychology in Society*, 25 (1999).

—'Time and learning', *South African Journal of Psychology*, 30/4 (2000), 6–16.

—'Culture and knowledge', *South African Journal of Philosophy*, 20/2 (2001), 191–214.

—'Education and the question about understanding', *South African Journal of Higher Education*, 15/1 (2001), 25–31.

—'Culture and the individual', *Theory and Psychology*, 13/5 (2003), 629–50.

—*What is the Self? A Philosophy of Psychology* (Lewiston: The Edwin Mellen Press, Ltd, 2006).

—and Beishuizen, J.J., 'Psychological testing in a multicultural society: Universal or particular competencies', *Intercultural Education*, 13/2 (2002), 201–13.

—and Bradbury, J.L., *A Guide to Learning* (Kenwyn: Juta and Co. Ltd, 1994).

—and Kernoff, R.J., 'An analysis of underprepared students' developing textual interpretation', *South African Journal of Higher Education*, 9/1 (1995), 23–30.

—and Winter, P.A., 'An analysis of learners' engagement in mathematical tasks', *South African Journal of Higher Education*, 4/1 (1990), 59–68.

—and Winter, P.A., 'The meta- and epistemic constraints on praxis: The learning-teaching dialectic in mathematics', *Perspectives in Education*, 13/1 (1991–2), 45–67.

—Griesel, H. and Witz. L., *Conceptual Dictionary* (Kenwyn: Juta and Co. Ltd, 1994).

Cristensen, W., 'Self-directedness, integration and higher cognition', *Language Sciences*, 26 (2004), 661–92

Cummins, D.D. and Cummins, R., 'Biological preparedness and evolutionary explanation', *Cognition*, 73/3 (1999), 37–53.

Damasio, H., Grabowski, T.J., Tranel, D., Hichwa, R.D. and Damasio, A.R., 'A neural basis for lexical retrieval', *Nature*, 380 (1996), 449–505.

Dancy, J., *Introduction to Contemporary Epistemology* (Oxford: Basil Blackwell, 1989).

D'Andrade, R.G., 'The cultural part of cognition', *Cognitive Science*, 5 (1981), 179–95.

Dawkins, R., *The Ancestor's Tale* (London: Weidenfeld and Nicolson, 2004).

Deary, I.J., 'Individual differences in cognition: British contributions over a century', *British Journal of Psychology*, 92 (2001), 217–37.

—and Caryl, P.G., 'Neuroscience and human intelligence', *Trends in Neuroscience*, 20/8 (1998), 365–71.

Demetriou, A., 'NOOPLASIS: 10 + 1 postulates about the formation of the mind', Special issue of *Learning and Instruction: The Journal of the European Association for Research in Learning and Instruction*, 8/4 (1998).

Dennett, D.C., *Consciousness Explained* (London: Penguin, 1991).

—*Darwin's Dangerous Idea. Evolution and the Meanings of Life* (London: Penguin, 1995).

—*Kinds of Minds* (London: Weidenfeld and Nicolson, 1996).

—*Freedom Evolves* (London: Penguin, 2004).

Derwing, B.L., *Transformational Grammar as a Theory of Language Acquisition* (Cambridge: CUP, 1973).

Diamond, J., *Collapse. How Societies Choose to Fail or Succeed* (New York: Viking, 2005).

Eco, U., *Kant and the Platypus* (London: Secker and Warburg, 1999).

Eysenck, H.J., *The Structure of Human Personality* (New York: Wiley, 1953).

Fabricius, W.V., 'Piaget's theory of knowledge. Its philosophical context', *Human Development*, 26 (1983), 325–34.

Feldman, D.H. and Fowler, R.C., 'The nature(s) of developmental change: Piaget, Vygotsky, and the transition process', *New Ideas in Psychology*, 15/3 (1998), 195–210.

Feuerstein, R., *The Dynamic Assessment of Retarded Performers* (Baltimore: University Park Press, 1979).

—Rand, Y., Hoffman, M.B. and Miller, R., *Instrumental Enrichment. An Intervention Program for Cognitive Modifiability* (Baltimore: University Park Press, 1980).

Feyerabend, P., *Against Method* (Bristol: Western Printing Services Ltd, 1975).

Friedman, T., *The World is Flat: A Brief History of the Twenty-first Century* (New York: Farrar, Strauss and Giroux, 2005).

Fodor, J.A., *The Language of Thought* (Cambridge, MA: Harvard University Press, 1970).

—*Representations* (Cambridge, MA: MIT Press, 1981).

—*Psychosemantics* (Cambridge, MA: MIT Press, 1987).

—*In Critical Condition. Polemical Essays on Cognitive Science and the Philosophy of Mind* (Cambridge, MA: The MIT Press, 1998).

—*The Mind Doesn't Work That Way. The Scope and Limits of Computational Psychology* (Cambridge, MA: The MIT Press, 2001).

— *A Theory of Content and Other Essays* (Cambridge, MA: MIT Press, 2002).

Funder, D.C., 'Personality', *Annual Review of Psychology*, 52 (2001), 197–221.

Ganzach, Y., 'Parents' education, cognitive ability, educational expectations and educational attainment: Interactive effects', *British Journal of Educational Psychology*, 70 (2000), 419–41.

Gardner, H., *Frames of Mind: The Theory of Multiple Intelligences* (New York: Basic Books, 1983).

—*Creating Minds* (New York: Basic Books, 1993)

—*Multiple Intelligences: The Theory into Practice* (New York: Basic Books, 1993).

—*Intelligence Reframed: Multiple Intelligences for the 21st Century* (New York: Basic Books, 1999).

—'The New New Math', *New York Review of Books*, 45/14 (24 September 1998).

143

Gazzaniga, M.S., Ivry, R.B., and Mangun, G.R., *Cognitive Neuroscience* (New York: Norton, 2002).

Geertz, C., *Local Knowledge. Further Essays in Interpretative Anthropology* (New York: Basic Books, 1983).

Gibson, J.J., 'The theory of affordances', in Shaw, R. and Bransford, J. (eds.), *Perceiving, Acting and Knowing: Towards an Ecological Psychology* (New Jersey: Lawrence Erlbaum Associates, Inc., 1977).

Giddens, A., *The Consequences of Modernity* (Cambridge: Polity Press, 1992).

Goodhart, D., 'Too diverse?', *Prospect* (February 2004), 30–7.

Graham, G., 'Behaviorism', in Zalta, E.N (ed.), *The Stanford Encyclopedia of Philosophy* (Fall 2002 Edition).

Green, C.D., 'Where did the word "cognitive" come from anyway?', *Canadian Psychology*, 37 (1996), 31–9.

Greenfield, S., *The Human Brain. A Guided Tour* (London: Phoenix, 1997).

Grigorenko, E.L. and Sternberg, R.J., 'Dynamic testing', *Psychological Bulletin*, 124/1 (1998), 75–111.

Guttman, A. (ed.), *Multiculturalism* (Princeton, NJ: Princeton University Press, 1994).

Haack, S., *Evidence and Inquiry. Towards Reconstruction in Epistemology* (Oxford: Blackwell, 1995).

—*Manifesto of a Passionate Moderate* (Chicago: University of Chicago Press, 1998).

Hacking, I., *The Social Construction of What?* (Cambridge, MA: Harvard University Press, 1999).

Hamers, J.H.M., Sijtsma, K. and Riujssenaars, A.J.J.M., *Learning Potential Assessment. Theoretical, Methodological and Practical Issues* (Amsterdam: Swets and Zeitlinger, 1993).

Hermer-Vazquez, L., Spelke, E. and Katsnelson, A.S., 'Sources of flexibility in human cognition: Dual-task studies of space and language', *Cognitive Psychology*, 39 (1999), 3–36.

Herrnstein, R.J. and Murray, C., *The Bell Curve: Intelligence and Class Structure in American Life* (New York: The Free Press, 1994).

Hogan, R. and Roberts, B.W., 'Personality measurement and employment decisions', *American Psychologists*, 51/2 (1996), 469–77.

Hoggart, R., *The Way We Live Now* (London: Chatto and Windus, 1995).

144

Holt, J., 'Measure fore measure. The strange science of Francis Galton', *The New Yorker* (24 January 2005), 84–90.

Horvath, C.D., 'Interactionism and innateness in the evolutionary study of human nature', *Biology and Philosophy*, 15 (2000), 321–37.

Hutchins, E., *Cognition in the Wild* (Cambridge, MA: The MIT Press, 1995).

Jensen, A.R., *Bias in Mental Testing* (London: Methuen, 1980).

—*The G Factor. The Science of Mental Ability* (London: Praeger, 1998).

—'Jensen on "Jensenism"', *Intelligence*, 26/3 (1998), 181–208.

Karmiloff-Smith, A., 'Development itself is the key to understanding developmental disorders', *Trends in Cognitive Science*, 2/10 (1998), 389–98.

Kim, J., *Supervenience and Mind* (Cambridge: CUP, 1993).

—'Multiple realization and the metaphysics of reduction', *Philosophy and Phenomenological Research*, 52 (1992), 1–26.

Kirsh, D., 'Adapting the environment instead of oneself', *Adaptive Behavior*, 4/3/4 (1996), 415–52.

Kitchener, R.F., *Piaget's* Theory of Knowledge. *Genetic Epistemology and Scientific Reason* (New Haven: Yale University Press, 1986).

Koertge, N. (ed.), *A House Built on Sand. Exposing Postmodernist Myths about Science* (Oxford: OUP, 2000).

Kozulin, A. (ed.), *The Ontogeny of Cognitive Modifiability. Applied Aspects of Mediated Learning Experience and Instrumental Enrichment.* Proceedings of the International Conference (Jerusalem: ICELP, 1997).

Kuhn, D., *The Skills of Argument* (Cambridge: CUP, 1991).

—'Science as argument: Implications for teaching and learning scientific thinking', *Science Education*, 77/3 (1993), 319–37.

—'Is good thinking scientific thinking?', in Olson, D.R. and Torrance, N., *Modes of Thought. Explorations in Culture and Cognition* (Cambridge: CUP, 1996), 261–81.

Kuhn, T.S., *The Structure of Scientific Revolutions*, 2nd edn., enlarged (Chicago: University of Chicago Press, 1970).

LeDoux, J., *Synaptic Self. How Our Brains Become Who We Are* (London, Penguin, 2002).

Lefkowitz, M., *Not out of Africa. How Afrocentricism Became an Excuse to Teach Myth as History* (New York: Basic Books, 1997).

Leiderman, P.H., Babu, B., Kagia, J., Kraener, H.C. and Leiderman, G.F., 'African infant precocity and some social influences during the first year', *Nature*, 242/5395 (1973), 247–9.

Levin, J., 'Functionalism', in Zalta, E.N. (ed.), *The Stanford Encyclopedia of Philosophy* (Fall 2004 Edition).

Lloyd, E., 'Evolutionary psychology: The burdens of proof', *Biology and Philosophy*, 14 (1999), 211–33.

Lloyd, G.E.R., *Polarity and Analogy* (Cambridge: CUP, 1966).

—*Magic, Reason and Experience* (Cambridge: CUP, 1979).

—*The Revolutions of Wisdom* (Berkeley: Berkeley University Press, 1987).

—*Demystifying Mentalities* (Cambridge: CUP, 1990).

—*Adversaries and Authorities* (Cambridge: CUP, 1996).

Lubinski, D., 'Scientific and social significance of assessing individual differences: "Sinking shafts at a few critical points"', *Annual Review of Psychology*, 51 (2000), 405–44.

Luria, A.R., *Cognitive Development. Its Cultural and Social Foundations* (Cambridge, MA: Harvard University Press, 1976).

—*The Making of Mind. A Personal Account of Soviet Psychology*, Cole, M. and Cole, S. (eds.) (Cambridge, MA: Harvard University Press, 1979).

Luther, M., Cole, E. and Gamlin, P., *Dynamic Assessment for Instruction. From Theory to Application* (York, CA: Captus University Press, 1996).

MacIntyre, A., *After Virtue. A Study in Moral Theory* (London: Duckworth, 1992).

Mameli, M., 'Modules and Mindreaders', *Biology and Philosophy*, 16 (2001), 377–93.

Maravita, A. and Iriki, A., 'Tools for the body (schema)', *Trends in Cognitive Science*, 8/2 (2004), 79–86.

Marcus, G.F., 'Can connectionism save constructivism?', *Cognition*, 66/2 (1998), 153–82.

Markie, P., 'Rationalism vs. Empiricism', in Zalta, E.N. (ed.), *The Stanford Encyclopedia of Philosophy* (Fall 2004 Edition).

Markman, A.B. and Gentner, D., 'Thinking', *Annual Review of Psychology*, 52 (2000), 223–47.

Merleau-Ponty, M., *Phenomenology of Perception*, trans. R.C. McCleary (New York: Routledge and Kegan Paul, 1965).

Millikan, R.G., *Language, Thought, and other Biological Categories* (Cambridge, MA: The MIT Press, 1984).

—*White Queen Psychology and Other Essays for Alice* (Cambridge, MA: The MIT Press, 1995).

—'Pushmi-pullyu representations', *Philosophical Perspectives*, 9 (1995), 185–200.

Mischel, W., *Personality and Assessment* (New York: Wiley, 1968).

Morphet, T., Lazarus, J. and Hunter, P., 'General conclusion', *South African Journal of Higher Education*, 3/1 (1989), 172.

Nagel, T., *The View from Nowhere* (Oxford: OUP, 1986).

Nagel, T., *The Last Word* (Oxford: OUP, 1997).

Neander, K., 'Teleological theories of mental content', in Zalta E.N. (ed.), *The Stanford Encyclopedia of Philosophy* (Summer 2004 Edition).

Norbert, E., *The Civilizing Process. The History of Manners and State Formation and Civilization* (Oxford: Blackwell, 1997).

Ogbu, J.U., 'Origins of human competence: A cultural-ecological perspective', *Child Development*, 52 (1981), 413–29.

—and Stern, P., 'Caste status and intellectual development', in Sternberg, R.J. and Grigorenko, E.L. (eds.), *Environmental Effects on Cognitive Abilities* (New Jersey: Lawrence Erlbaum Associates, Inc., 1994), 1–37.

O'Neill, O., *Towards Justice and Virtue. A Constructive Account of Practical Reasoning* (Cambridge: CUP, 1996).

—*Bounds of Justice* (Cambridge: CUP, 2000).

Pascual-Leone, J., 'Attentional, dialectic, and mental effort: Toward an organismic theory of life-stages', in Commons, M.L., Richards, F.A. and Armon, A.C. (eds.), *Beyond Formal Operations: Late Adolescent and Adult Cognitive Development* (New York: Praeger, 1984).

—'Organism processes for neo-Piagetian theories: A dialectical causal account of cognitive development', *International Journal of Psychology*, 22 (1987), 531–70.

—'Vygotsky, Piaget, and the problem of Plato', *Swiss Journal of Psychology*, 55/2/3 (1996), 84–96.

—and Goodman, D., *Intelligence and Experience: A Neo-Piagetian Approach. Report No. 81* (York, Ontario: York University, Department of Psychology, June 1979).

—and Baillargeon, R., 'Developmental measurement of mental attention', *International Journal of Behavioural Development*, 17/1 (1994), 161–200.

Paunonen, S.V. and Ashton, M.C., 'Big five factors and facets and the prediction of behaviour', *Journal of Personality and Social Psychology*, 81/3 (2001), 524–39.

Piaget, J., *The Psychology of Intelligence* (New Jersey: Littlefield, Adams and Co., 1976).

—*The Development of Thought*, trans. A. Rosin (Oxford: Basil Blackwell, 1977).

—*Adaptation and Intelligence: Organic Selection and Phenocopy* (Chicago: University of Chicago Press, 1980).

Piatelli-Palmarini, M., *Language and Learning. The Debate between Jean Piaget and Noam Chomsky* (London: Routledge and Kegan Paul, 1980).

—'Evolution, selection and cognition: From "learning" to parameter setting in biology and in the study of language', *Cognition*, 31 (1989), 1–44.

Pinker, S., *The Language Instinct* (New York: Harper Collins, 1994).

—*How the Mind Works* (London: Penguin, 1997).

—*The Blank Slate* (London: Penguin, 2002).

Plotkin, H., *The Imagined World Made Real* (London: Penguin, 2003).

Prasada, S., 'Acquiring generic knowledge', *Trends in Cognitive Science*, 4/2 (2000), 66–72.

Pylyshyn, Z., 'The role of competence theories in cognitive psychology', *The Journal of Psycholinguistics*, 2/1 (1973), 21–50.

Quartz, S.R., 'The constructivist brain', *Trends in Cognitive Science* 3/2 (1999), 48–57.

—and Sejnowski, T.J., 'The neural basis of cognitive development: A constructivist manifesto', *Behavioral and Brain Sciences*, 20 (1997), 537–96.

Rachlin, H., *The Science of Self-control* (Cambridge, MA: Harvard University Press, 2000).

Resing, W.C.M. and van Wijk, A.M., 'Leerpotentieel: Onderzoek bij allochtone leerlingen uit het basisonderwijs', *Tijdschrift voor Orthopedagogiek*, 35 (1996), 432–44.

Ridley, M., *Nature via Nurture. Genes, Experience and What Makes Us Human* (London: Harper Perennial, 2003).

Rorty, R., *Truth and Progress. Philosophical Papers* (Cambridge: CUP, 1998).

Rosin, H., 'God and country', *The New Yorker* (27 June 2003).

Ross, D. and Spurrett, D., 'What to say to a sceptical metaphysician: A defense manual for cognitive and behavioural scientists', *Behavioral and Brain Sciences*, 27/5 (2004), 603–27.

Rowlands, M., *The Body in Mind. Understanding Cognitive Processes* (Cambridge: CUP, 1999).

Rushton, J.P., 'The "Jensen Effect" and the "Spearman-Jensen Hypothesis" of black-white IQ differences', *Intelligence*, 26/3 (1998), 217–25.

Searle, J.R., *The Mystery of Consciousness* (New York: A *New York Review* Book, 1997).

Shapin, S., *The Scientific Revolution* (Chicago: University of Chicago Press, 1996).

Silverman, I. and Eals, M., 'Sex differences in spatial abilities: Evolutionary theory and data', in Barkow, J.H., Cosmides, L. and Tooby, J. (eds.), *The Adapted Mind. Evolutionary Psychology and the Generation of Culture* (Oxford: OUP, 1992), 533–53.

Simons, D.J. and Chabris, C.F., 'Gorillas in our midst: Sustained inattentional blindness for dynamic events', *Perception*, 28 (1999), 1059–74.

Skinner, B.F., *Verbal Behavior* (New York: Appleton-Century-Crofts, 1957).

Smith, L., 'A constructivist interpretation of formal operations', *Human Development*, 30 (1987), 341–54.

—'Internality of mental representation. Twenty questions for interactivism', *Consciousness and Emotion*, 4/2 (2003), 307–26.

Snow, R.E., 'Individual differences in the design of educational programs', *American Psychologists*, 41/10 (1986), 1029–39.

Sokal, A. and Bricmont, J., *Fashionable Nonsense. Postmodern Intellectuals' Abuse of Science* (New York: Picador, 1998).

Spelke, E., 'Initial knowledge: Six suggestions', *Cognition*, 50 (1994), 431–45.

Stankov, L., 'The theory of fluid and crystallized intelligence. New findings and recent developments', *Learning and Individual Differences*, 12/1 (2000), 1–3.

Sternberg, R., *The Triarchic Mind. A New Theory of Intelligence* (New York: Viking Press, 1988).

Strohm-Kitchener, K., 'Cognition, metacognition, and epistemic cognition. A three-level model of cognitive processing', *Human Development*, 26 (1983), 222–32.

Tattersall, I., 'Once we were not alone', *Scientific American* (25 August 2003), 20–27.

Taylor, C., *Human Agency and Language. Philosophical Papers 1* (Cambridge: CUP, 1992).

Thagard, P., 'Cognitive Science', in Zalta, E.N. (ed.), *The Stanford Encyclopedia of Philosophy* (Winter 2004 Edition).

Thelen, E. and Smith, L., *A Dynamic Systems Approach to the Development of Cognition in Action* (Cambridge, MA: The MIT Press, 1994).

Thomas, M., 'Quo vadis modularity in the 1990s', *Learning and Individual Differences*, 10/3 (1998), 245–50.

Toulmin, S., *Cosmopolis. The Hidden Agenda of Modernity* (New York: The Free Press, 1990).

Valsiner, J., *The Guided Mind. A Sosiogenetic Approach to Personality* (Cambridge, MA: Harvard University Press, 1998).

—*Culture and Human Development: An Introduction* (London: Sage, 2000).

Vosniadou, S., 'Towards a revised cognitive psychology for new advances in learning and instruction', *Learning and Instruction*, 6/2 (1996), 95–109.

—Ioannides, C., Dimitakopoulou, A. and Papademetriou, E., 'Designing learning environments to promote conceptual change in science', *Learning and Instruction*, 11/4–5 (2001), 381–419.

Vuyk, R., *Overview and Critique of Piaget's Genetic Epistemology 1965–1980. Volumes One and Two* (London: Academic Press, 1981).

Vygotsky, L.S., *Mind in Society. The Development of Higher Psychological Processes*, Cole, M., John-Steiner, V., Scribner, S. and Souberman, E. (eds.) (Cambridge, MA: Harvard University Press, 1978).

Walter, N., 'Prejudice and evolution', *Prospect* (June 2005), 34–9.

Weinberg, S., 'The revolution that didn't happen', *New York Review of Books* (8 October 1998), 48–52.

Wertsch, J., *Culture, Communication and Cognition* (Cambridge: CUP, 1985).

Williams, M., *Unnatural Doubts. Epistemological Realism and the Basis of Scepticism* (Princeton, NJ: Princeton University Press, 1996).

—'Understanding human knowledge philosophically', *Philosophy and Phenomenological Research*, LVI/2 (1996), 359–79.

Willingham, D.T., 'Reframing the mind: Howard Gardner became a hero among educators simply by redefining talents as "intelligences"', *Education Next* (Summer 2004).

Wilson, E.O., *Consilience. The Unity of Knowledge* (London: Abacus, 1998).

Wilson, M. and Daly, M., 'Do pretty women inspire men to discount the future?', *Proceedings of the Royal Society of London, Supplementary – Biology Letters* (2003), 271, S177–9.

Winch, P., *The Idea of a Social Science* (London: Routledge and Kegan Paul, 1970).

150

Wolcott, J., 'Caution: Women seething', *Vanity Fair* (June 2005), 64.

Wolpert, L., *The Unnatural Nature of Science* (Cambridge, MA: Harvard University Press, 1997).

Wynn, T. and Coolidge, F.L., 'The expert Neandertal mind', *Journal of Human Evolution*, 46 (2003), 467–87.

WEB SITES CONSULTED

Chapter 1

http://www.findarticles.com/p/articles/mi_m2185/is_3_14/ai_99430630/print

http://www.epistemelinks.com/Main/Philosophers.aspx?PhilCode=Fano

http://www.marxists.org/reference/subject/philosophy/works/ot/fanon.htm

http://www.pipeline.com/~rgibson/FANON.htm

http://www.zonalatina.com/Zldata288.htm

http://www.findarticles.com/p/articles/mi_qa3935/is_200304/ai_n9181266#contin
ue

http://www.findarticles.com/p/search?qt=paulo+freire&qf=free&tb=art

http://www.washingtonpost.com/wp-
srv/national/longterm/meltingpot/melt0222.htm

http://news.bbc.co.uk/1/hi/world/europe/3619988.stm

http://islam.about.com/cs/currentevents/i/france_hijab.htm

http://www.cnn.com/US/9908/12/kansas.evolution.flap/

http://www.abanet.org/irr/hr/yared.html

http://www.tes.co.uk/section/staffroom/thread.aspx?story_id=2068824&path=/sco
tland/scotland+-+opinion/&threadPage=1

http://www.questia.com/search/cultural-history-education

http://www.questia.com/PM.qst?a=o&d=54447684.

http://www.gpsworld.com/gpsworld/

http://etext.lib.virginia.edu/cgi-local/DHI/dhi.cgi?id=dv2-08

http://www.ecotopia.com/webpress/deschooling.htm

http://www.deschooling.org/

http://www.lblp.com/downloads/PDF/research/Gestalt.pdf

http://www--distance.syr.edu/pvitapf.html

http://www.paulofreire.org/

Chapter 2

http://www.findarticles.com/p/articles/mi_m0JVP/is_2002_Winter/ai_97483140

http://www.psy.pdx.edu/PsiCafe/KeyTheorists/Sternberg.htm#Papers

http://www.eiconsortium.org/

http://www.findarticles.com/p/articles/mi_m0MJG/is_3_4/ai_n6143580#continue

http://www.pz.harvard.edu/PIs/HGpubs.htm

http://www.findarticles.com/p/articles/mi_qa3671/is_200401/ai_n9380545/

http://plato.stanford.edu/archives/spr2004/entries/epistemology-evolutionary/

http://en.wikipedia.org/w/index.php?title=Special:Allpages&from=Apple_propag ation

http://www.apa.org/about/

http://www.bps.org.uk/

http://etext.lib.virginia.edu/cgi-local/DHI/dhi.cgi?id=dv2-08

http://www.ornl.gov/sci/techresources/Human_Genome/home.shtml

http://www.ornl.gov/sci/techresources/Human_Genome/elsi/cloning.shtml#whatis

Chapter 3

http://plato.stanford.edu/entries/cognitive–science/

http://cogweb.ucla.edu/CogSci/Spelke.html

http://plato.stanford.edu/archives/fall2002/entries/behaviorism/

http://eclectic.ss.uci.edu/~drwhite/Anthro179a/DistributedCognition.pdf

http://www.cogs.susx.ac.uk/users/ronc/papers/embodiment.pdf

http://arjournals.annualreviews.org/doi/abs/10.1146/annurev.neuro.27.070203.144 230

http://www.brainconnection.com/content/181_1

http://plato.stanford.edu/archives/win2002/entries/neuroscience/

http://findarticles.com/p/articles/mi_qa3671/is_200401/ai_n9380531

http://www.ornl.gov/sci/techresources/Human_Genome/elsi/cloning.shtml#whatis

http://www.roslin.ac.uk/public/cloning.html

http://www.ornl.gov/sci/techresources/Human_Genome/home.shtml

152

http://stemcells.nih.gov/index.asp

http://www.africagenome.co.za

http://plato.stanford.edu/archives/sum2004/entries/content-teleological/

http://www.intriguing.com/mp/_scripts/matchtie.asp

http://plato.stanford.edu/archives/fall2004/entries/functionalism/

http://people.csail.mit.edu/brooks/

http://whyfiles.org/siegfried/story01/

Chapter 4

http://findarticles.com/p/articles/mi_qa3671/is_200401

http://anthro.palomar.edu/social/default.htm

http://www.personalityresearch.org/

http://www.acf.hhs.gov/programs/hsb/

http://www.uwex.edu/news/story.cfm/523

http://www.fpg.unc.edu/~abc/

http://plato.stanford.edu/archives/fall2004/entries/rationalism-empiricism/

http://cogweb.ucla.edu/CogSci/Spelke.html

http://plato.stanford.edu/archives/fall2002/entries/behaviorism/

http://plato.stanford.edu/archives/spr2004/entries/epistemology-evolutionary/

Chapter 5

http://findarticles.com/p/articles/mi_qa3671/is_200401

http://www.questia.com/search/cultural-history-education

http://www.questia.com/PM.qst?a=o&d=54447684

http://www.findarticles.com/p/articles/mi_m0JVP/is_2002_Winter/ai_97483140

INDEX

154

156